RAISING
LATTER-DAY
STRIPLING
WARRIORS

5 STRATEGIES FOR BUILDING A FORMIDABLE FAMILY FORTRESS

DEBBIE BOWEN

CFI
An Imprint of Cedar Fort, Inc.
Springville, Utah

This is not an official publication of The Church of Jesus Christ of Latter-day Saints. The opinions and views expressed herein belong solely to the author and do not necessarily represent the opinions or views of Cedar Fort, Inc. Permission for the use of sources, graphics, and photos is also solely the responsibility of the author.

ISBN 13: 978-1-4621-1870-0

Published by CFI, an imprint of Cedar Fort, Inc.
2373 W. 700 S., Springville, UT 84663
Distributed by Cedar Fort, Inc., www.cedarfort.com

LIBRARY OF CONGRESS CATALOGING-IN-PUBLICATION DATA

Names: Bowen, Debbie, 1962- author.
Title: Raising latter-day stripling warriors / Debbie Bowen.
Description: Springville, Utah : CFI, An imprint of Cedar Fort, Inc., [2016]
| "2016 | Includes bibliographical references and index. | Description
based on print version record and CIP data provided by publisher; resource
not viewed.
Identifiers: LCCN 2015048471 (print) | LCCN 2015047909 (ebook) | ISBN
9781462126613 () | ISBN 9781462118700 (perfect bound : alk. paper)
Subjects: LCSH: Mormon youth. | Mormon families. | Child rearing--Religious
aspects--Church of Jesus Christ of Latter-day Saints. | Child
rearing--Religious aspects--Mormon Church. | Parent and child--Religious
aspects--Church of Jesus Christ of Latter-day Saints. | Parent and
child--Religious aspects--Mormon Church.
Classification: LCC BX8643.Y6 (print) | LCC BX8643.Y6 B69 2016 (ebook) | DDC
248.8/45088289332--dc23
LC record available at http://lccn.loc.gov/2015048471

Cover design by Shawnda T. Craig
Cover design © 2016 Cedar Fort, Inc.

Printed in the United States of America

10 9 8 7 6 5 4 3 2 1

Printed on acid-free paper

Dear Latter-day General,

Do you find yourself feeling overwhelmed by Satan's relentless assaults on the family? And does it seem like you are fighting an uphill battle when it comes to raising righteous children and prioritizing your life? Building spiritual armor and a formidable fortress are essential elements in defending your family against the demons of darkness.

As a lifelong commissioned officer in God's army and His trusted emissary, it is your sacred duty to lead your own mini militia in the march for truth and light. I salute you for your determination to stay the course, despite incredible odds. It is my hope that the crucial strategies outlined within these pages will aid you in your search for greater peace and purpose.

This book is for all types of generals—traditional parents, single parents, stepparents, grandparents—anyone responsible for nurturing the next generation of soldiers. Raising righteous latter-day warriors is the great quest of parenthood.

Godspeed—

Other Books by Debbie Bowen

From Pampered to Productive—Raising Children Who Know How to Work (originally titled W.O.R.K.: Wonderful Opportunities for Raising Responsible Kids)

Nobody's Better Than You, Mom

Simply Sane: Living Outside the Fast Lane

Table of Contents

Contents

Stripling Warriors

Stripling Warriors

"I have no greater joy than to hear
that my children walk in truth."

—3 John 1:4

As I happily went about my work one day, my precocious, energetic six-year-old son bounded into the room and declared cavalierly, "I am going to choose the wrong." Alarms sounded in my head! What could have prompted such an unexpected decision?

"Why would you want to choose the wrong?" I wondered out loud.

"Because," he replied impishly, "then I can do practically anything I want."

And so, the battle for their souls begins . . .

Raising righteous children in today's world is a daunting endeavor, requiring extreme vigilance, for Satan rules his kingdom with turmoil and terror. The entire mission of the legions under his command is to diffuse and destroy and annul and annihilate anything that is "virtuous, lovely, or of good report or praiseworthy" (Articles of Faith 1:13). As evil escalates, our primary role as parents is to protect our precious offspring from Satan's assaults.

Our Latter-Day Battle

Like it or not, we are at war! We are in the midst of a rivalry that has been raging since before the beginning of time. It is a "vicious war for the souls of young and old alike, and the casualty count is climbing."[1] But this is not a battle of bullets and bombs and bayonets. This is a contest of light versus dark, right versus wrong, the Savior versus Satan. "For we wrestle not against flesh and blood, but against principalities, against powers, against the rulers of . . . darkness . . . against spiritual wickedness in high places" (Ephesians 6:12).

In the Grand Council in Heaven, when Satan rebelled against God and sought to defeat His plan, battle lines were drawn as the forces of good and evil aligned against each other. "And there was war in heaven: Michael and his angels fought against the dragon; and the dragon fought and his angels, and prevailed not; neither was their place found any more in heaven" (Revelation 12:7–8). Therefore, Satan "maketh war with the saints of God, and encompasseth them round about" (D&C 76:29).

"That struggle has not ended, only shifted battlegrounds. It is ruthless and relentless."[2] In these winding-up scenes of the longest war ever waged, Satan has launched his biggest campaign yet. The battle plan is in place; the strategies are set. He has had millennia to master his maneuvers and has a vast arsenal at his disposal. "Thus he goeth up and down, to and fro in the earth, seeking to destroy the souls of men" (D&C 10:27).

"O that cunning plan of the evil one!" (2 Nephi 9:28). Satan knows he ultimately loses the war; but he is determined to win as many personal battles as possible, and he will attempt to win at all costs. In this last-ditch effort to control and conquer, no technique is too extreme and no person is exempt. This is a war without rules or restrictions, and Satan never willingly retreats. He knows that if he can get our children while they are young, the chances of defection are slim. Therefore, we must begin at birth to prepare them for battle with this most brutal enemy. As always, the best defense is a good offense.

Building a Defense

A popular children's fairy tale emphasizes the importance of being prepared. When the three little pigs set out to find their fortunes, two of them, in shortsighted fashion, quickly threw together shabbily made huts that proved too flimsy to withstand the destructive blows of the big bad wolf. While his brothers played and fiddled, however, the third little pig toiled tirelessly. Because the wily wolf already had the advantage, no half-hearted, hasty attempt would provide the necessary protection from this menacing marauder. Brick by brick, the little pig labored diligently to build a formidable fortress. He knew his life depended on the quality of his workmanship.

Similarly, Satan lies at the thresholds of our doors. Therefore, we must prepare places of refuge from the forces of evil that threaten to destroy our families. The devil and his minions already have the upper hand, so this is no time for shortcuts or laziness. No half-hearted, passive attempts will provide the necessary protection from the proverbial predators prowling on our porches. Our families' spiritual lives hang in the balance. Procrastination or failure to adequately prepare only increases the probability that we perish. Brick by brick, day by day, year after year, we must build a fortress that will withstand the threatening blows of the demons at our doors. It is never too early to implement a defense strategy for your family.

Valiant Youth

Don't underestimate your children's ability to be valiant. "The Lord [will bless them] with wisdom beyond [their] years."[3] The scriptures contain many stories of young people who remained faithful despite difficult circumstances. Esther was a young Jewish maiden when crowned queen of Persia, but her unflinching faith and courage saved her people. During the time of Abraham, Pharaoh's priest offered up "three virgins at one time" because "they would not bow down to worship gods of wood or of stone" (Abraham 1:11). And the "damsel" (Genesis 24:16) Rebekah left her family to marry a man she had never met, trusting her future life to the Lord.

Relatively speaking, Enoch was "but a lad" when he was called to preach repentance (Moses 6:31). "And so great was the faith of Enoch that he led the people of God, and their enemies came to battle against them; and he spake the word of the Lord, and the earth trembled, and the mountains fled, . . . and the rivers of water were turned out of their course," and "the Lord came and dwelt with his people" (Moses 7:13, 16). Eventually, they became so righteous that the entire city was taken up to heaven (see Moses 7:21).

When Daniel, Shadrach, Meshach, and Abed-nego were taken captive by the Babylonians, they refused to participate in the worldly practices of their peers—and they prospered. "As for these four children, God gave them knowledge and skill in all learning and wisdom: and . . . [the king] found them ten times better than all the magicians and astrologers that were in all his realm" (Daniel 1:17, 20). Later, when faced with almost certain death in a fiery furnace, Shadrach, Meshach, and Abed-nego refused to worship the golden idol that King Nebuchadnezzar had caused to be erected (see Daniel 3). And when Daniel was threatened with death in a den of lions if he prayed to God, "he went into his house; and his windows being open in his chamber . . . kneeled upon his knees three times a day, and prayed, and gave thanks before his God, as he did aforetime" (Daniel 6:10).

Jacob's son Joseph was just seventeen when his brothers sold him to a traveling caravan to be taken to Egypt as a slave. He remained true to his beliefs while living far from home and family (see Genesis 37). At age thirty, he became ruler over all the land—second only to Pharaoh (see Genesis 41:40–46).

Joseph Smith was but an "obscure boy" (Joseph Smith—History 1:22) of fourteen when he offered a prayer that completely changed the course of latter-day history. And when Jesus was only twelve years old, his parents found him at the temple, "sitting in the midst of the doctors, both hearing them, and asking them questions. And all that heard him were astonished at his understanding and answers" (Luke 2:46–47).

Nephi was "exceedingly young" (1 Nephi 2:16) when his family left Jerusalem, yet he was obedient in all he was asked to do. At age ten, Mormon was entrusted with the care and keeping of a thousand years of Nephite records, and at fifteen he was visited by the Lord (see Mormon 1:15). He was true to his convictions even though "a continual scene of wickedness and abominations [had] been before [his] eyes ever since [he had] been sufficient to behold the ways of man" (Mormon 2:18).

Moroni became captain of the entire Nephite army at only twenty-five. Despite great power and prominence, he never compromised his principles. Commenting on Moroni's integrity, Mormon said, "If all men had been, and were, and ever would be, like unto Moroni, behold, the very powers of hell would have been shaken forever; yea, the devil would never have power over the hearts of the children of men" (Alma 48:17).

The Original Stripling Warriors

The Book of Mormon describes in detail an army of "very young" soldiers (Alma 56:46). Though these stripling warriors fought with swords and cimeters, there are parallels for our *latter-day* stripling warriors, and we can learn critical combat strategies by studying their story.

First, it's important to remember that their *mothers* taught them—not the Primary, the Sunday School, their Young Men leaders, their bishops, the Missionary Training Center, their mission presidents, or their military leaders. Apparently, these righteous women had a battle plan of their own. As commanders in chief of their own mini militias, their homes became specialized boot camps where their children were taught and trained in religious tactical maneuvers. They did not wait for the ward to provide a defense strategy for their little bands of soldiers.

Day by day, these faithful mothers fashioned a "breastplate of righteousness," a "shield of faith," and a "helmet of salvation" (Ephesians 6:14, 16, 17) for each of their young warriors, and when the call to arms came, their sons were prepared. Two thousand young men marched into battle with their "loins girt about with truth" and their "feet shod with the preparation of the gospel of peace" (Ephesians 6:14–15). Indeed, they were protected with "the whole armour of God" (Ephesians 6:11).

In the conflicts of centuries past, adequate armor was essential. In fact, the breastplates, shields, and thick clothing with which Moroni outfitted his men were a great deterrent to the ill-clad Lamanite army when they came to battle. Even though the Lamanites greatly outnumbered the Nephites, they dared not engage in combat due to their own scarcity of protective attire (see Alma 43:21–22).

Second, these young men were taught while still in their youth. "Yea, they were men of truth and soberness, for they had been taught to keep the commandments of God and to walk uprightly before him" (Alma 53:21). "Yea, and they did obey and observe to perform every word of command with exactness; yea, and even according to their faith it was done unto them . . . and they [did] put their trust in God continually" (Alma 57:21, 27).

"Now they never had fought, yet they did not fear death; . . . yea, they had been taught by their mothers, that if they did not doubt, God would deliver them" (Alma 56:47). "And now, their preservation was astonishing. . . . And we do justly ascribe it to the miraculous power of God, because of their exceeding faith in that which they had been taught to believe" (Alma 57:25–26). Had their mothers waited until their sons were deployed to begin teaching, those battles could have proven fatal.

Third, their parents were remarkable role models. Years earlier, these righteous Lamanite parents were converted to the gospel of Jesus Christ. In honor of their covenant to never again shed the blood of others, they buried their weapons of war deep in the ground and "would suffer death in the most aggravating and distressing manner which could be inflicted by their brethren, before they would take the sword or cimeter to smite them" (Alma 27:29). Many of these parents, however, were spared the fatal blows of their Lamanite oppressors and went to live among the Nephites. "And they were . . . distinguished for their zeal towards God, and also towards men; for they were perfectly honest and upright in all things; and they were firm in the faith of Christ, even unto the end" (Alma 27:27). Without a doubt, the righteous teachings, powerful examples, and personal testimonies of these faithful parents left lasting impressions on their young sons.

The Influence of Righteous Parents

Other scriptural accounts also outline the important roles fathers have played. For example, Lehi was always teaching, and he "did exhort [his children] . . . with all the feeling of a tender parent" (1 Nephi 8:37).

And it was the words Enos had "often" heard his father speak "concerning eternal life, and the joy of the saints" that prompted a prayer that lasted all day and all night (Enos 1:3). His father's word "sunk deep into [his] heart," and his "soul hungered" to know the things his father knew (Enos 1:3–4). I wonder how many times his father spoke those words before they really made a difference for Enos.

Alma the Younger and the sons of King Mosiah turned

from being the "vilest of sinners" (Mosiah 28:4) in large part because Alma's father "prayed with much faith" (Mosiah 27:14). Alma later became the prophet and high priest of the Church. And, ironically, the sons of Mosiah were the missionaries who taught the parents of the stripling warriors.

Parents matter. Raising latter-day warriors is our greatest God-given responsibility, and the Lord expects our very best effort in this noble cause. We must practice "righteous, intentional parenting."[4] Getting down in the trenches and fighting side by side with our children can make all the difference.

Satan also recognizes the vital roles parents play. Because he knows the power of righteous mothers and fathers, "Satan has declared war on [parent]hood. He knows that those who rock the cradle can rock his earthly empire. And he knows that without righteous mothers [and fathers] loving and leading the next generation, the kingdom of God will fail. . . . As [parents] in Israel, we are the Lord's secret weapon. . . . [We must] rise to the challenge of being [parents] in these perilous times, though doing so may test the last ounce of [our] endurance and courage and faith."[5]

We must "work at our responsibility as parents as if everything in life counted on it, because in fact everything in life does count on it."[6] Our children are always watching, and we are always teaching. They notice discrepancies between our dedication to our favorite television programs and other lesser activities and the frequency and focus of family home evening, family prayer and scripture study, temple attendance, Sabbath day observance, payment of our tithes and offerings, our performance of Church callings, and our commitment to home and visiting teaching. "We must carefully continue to evaluate our performance as parents. The most powerful teaching a child will ever receive will come from concerned and righteous fathers and mothers. . . . There has never been a period . . . when our Father in Heaven's children have needed the guiding hand of faithful, devoted parents more."[7]

Just like the Ammonite women of long ago, mothers today are leaders. "In equal partnership with their husbands, they lead a great and eternal organization. [They] plan for the future of their organization. They plan for missions, temple marriages, and education. They plan for prayer, scripture study, and family home evening. . . . [They] build children into future leaders and are the primary examples of what leaders look like."[8] They know that "to bring up a child in the way he should go, [they must] travel that way [themselves]."[9]

As parent-generals over our own elite band of soldiers, we must devise a plan for leading the charge against sin and Satan, consistently teaching truth in an increasingly wicked world. Generals in God's army stand boldly at the head of their own beloved battalion. Because they know what is at stake, they do not back down, back off, or back away. They do not deviate from their battle plan.

My husband and I were blessed with six sons. Every time a baby boy was born, my husband would state matter-of-factly, "Another missionary." Then we earnestly set about trying to make it happen. We didn't just secretly hope they would serve missions. From the moment they entered mortality, we planned and prepared and taught and trained them for their eventual service as latter-day warriors in the greatest army ever assembled.

Our approach was not haphazard or random; it was deliberate. I realize that even the best-made plans sometimes go amiss, but not having a plan at all leaves everything to chance.

Making Our Home a Fortress

Our children are counting on us to keep them safe. Brick by brick, through regular family rituals, we can build a formidable fortress—not a citadel of mortar, brick, and stone, but, rather, a carefully constructed edifice of faith that provides increased protection from the adversary.

A faith-filled fortress has little to do with physical characteristics. In fact, many righteous Saints have come from humble places. I am sure Adam and Eve's first dwelling after being driven from the Garden of Eden was far from fashionable. And when referring to Lehi's wilderness abode, Nephi stated simply, "And my father dwelt in a tent" (1 Nephi 2:15). Abraham also described similar nomadic accommodations as he and Sarah "sojourned in the land of promise" (Hebrews 11:9) and "dwelt in tents as [they] came on [their] way" (Abraham 2:15).

More recently, many of our pioneer ancestors lived in dirt dugouts carved into hillsides; in cold, cramped cabins; or under covered wagon boxes. Their family fortresses were not defined by the strength and structure of their shelters, but instead on their firm foundation in Jesus Christ and a fervent desire to serve Him at all costs.

In fact, a fortress may not even be a place at all. When a devastating fire completely destroyed a family's house, a neighbor tried to comfort the seven-year-old son over the loss of his "home." The little guy thought a moment, and then said, "Oh, that's where you're mistaken. That wasn't our home; that was just our house. We still have our home; we just don't have any place to put it right now."[10] Talk about perspective!

Likewise, the style, size, and structure of our homes are irrelevant when it comes to providing a place of refuge for our families. Most of my family's early dwellings were anything but stylish. Our oldest child spent his first year in a cold, brightly wallpapered basement apartment, and when our two oldest were toddlers, we spent nine months as head residents of a noisy college dormitory while my husband completed an internship on campus. Like roaming nomads, we moved from place to place for the first eight years of our marriage as my husband's college career dictated. Still, we had religious devotionals in every placed we lived, and every *house* became a *home*.

Just eight months after painstakingly building our only new home, we sold it and moved to a little island in the middle of the Pacific Ocean. We spent the next three years living in a cinderblock house, painted white inside and out. Balmy breezes drifted daily through our open windows, but with those breezes came salty ocean air, wreaking havoc everywhere it settled—especially anything metal. In a profound way, I came to understand what the Savior meant when He said, "Lay not up for yourselves treasures upon earth, where moth and rust doth corrupt, and where thieves break through and steal. . . . For where your treasure is, there will your heart be also" (Matthew 6:19, 21). Earthly possessions became far less tempting when we realized how temporary they really were. Despite our modest accommodations, our family shared some of our most cherished memories while living in that little bungalow by the beach, and I will never regret what we gave up to make them happen.

Furthermore, my children have served missions in faraway places, where many of the homes are constructed of cardboard, corrugated tin, or scraps of wood—anything the people can find to keep out the wind and weather. In these simple circumstances, my children learned that an abundance of worldly goods does not make one wealthy. While working, living, and teaching among the poorest of the poor, they have come to know that "he that hath eternal life is rich" (D&C 6:7).

Fortifying our fortresses, therefore, is not a matter of finances but rather of refocusing our priorities. Years ago, Elder Gary E. Stevenson encouraged us to take a virtual tour of our homes with spiritual eyes:

> Imagine that you are opening your front door and walking inside your home. What do you see, and how do you feel? Is it a place of love, peace, and refuge from the world, as is the temple? Is it clean and orderly? As you walk through the rooms of your home, do you see uplifting images which include appropriate pictures of the temple and the Savior? Is your bedroom or sleeping area a place for personal prayer? Is your gathering area or kitchen a place where food is prepared and enjoyed together, allowing uplifting conversation and family time? Are scriptures found in a room where the family can study, pray, and learn together? Can you find your personal gospel study space? Does the music you hear or the entertainment you see, online or otherwise, offend the Spirit? Is the conversation uplifting and without contention? That concludes our tour. Perhaps you, as I, found a few spots that need some "home improvement"— hopefully not an "extreme home makeover."

Whether our living space is large or small, humble or

extravagant, there is a place for each of these gospel priorities in each of our homes.[11]

Maintaining Our Fortress

As part of an ongoing home-improvement effort, there are daily, weekly, monthly, and yearly tasks we perform to keep things neat and tidy—vacuuming, dusting, cleaning, weeding, washing, painting, and mowing, to name a few. Sometimes these tasks can be tedious, repetitious, or even boring. So why bother? Because we know that it is easier to keep up than catch up, and regularly doing these small and simple things keeps our lives running more smoothly. Routine repairs and maintenance keep out the weeds and dirt and clutter and help prevent a multitude of problems.

Similarly, routine religious repairs keep our spiritual strongholds in good condition. We have to constantly be on guard against any dirt, damage, or dangers that may sneak stealthily into our homes. The Internet, television, cell phones, books, magazines, and movies "are there as guests and should only be welcomed when they are appropriate for family enjoyment."[12] "We cannot play with Satan's fiery darts and not get burned. . . . If what we look at, read, listen to or choose to do does not meet the Lords standards . . . turn it off, rip it up, throw it out, and slam the door."[13]

The scriptures teach that "sin lieth at the door" (Moses 5:23)—down on the ground where no one notices. Rarely does the *master manipulator* come banging on our doors, huffing and puffing and threatening to blow them down. Often, he comes in so discreetly that we aren't even aware he is there.

One of my family's pets is an extremely clever barn cat who knows exactly which outside doors we will be exiting on cold winter mornings. Because she really wants to be where it is warm, she lies patiently by the door, waiting for it to open, and then quickly darts into the house before anyone can catch her. Satan too hides covertly at the corners of our cottage doors, waiting for just the slightest breach to slip silently inside.

The Savior, on the other hand, *stands* at the door and *knocks* (see Revelation 3:20). He will never force, sneak, coerce, trick, or manipulate. We must choose to let Him in.

Parents are the guardians of hearth and home. We are the keepers of the gate, the watchmen and women on the tower. We cannot wait to raise a warning voice until the enemy is upon us. As you take a tour of your fortress, notice where spiritual repairs are needed or where your guard has been let down, allowing sin to slip in. It is always better "to prepare and prevent than it is to repair and repent."[14]

Building Spiritual Armor

Providing a place of refuge, however, is not enough. Since our novice combatants regularly find themselves outside our fortress and our parental protection, we can ensure greater safety by constructing virtual armor for their daily battles. Through righteous teachings and examples, we can provide inner safeguards that will enable them to "stand against the wiles of the devil" and "quench all the fiery darts of the wicked" (Ephesians 6:11, 16). Like the mothers of the stripling warriors, we must outfit them with the whole armor of God and gird their loins with truth.

Historically, girding your loins was a familiar military phrase. Rarely used in modern times, much of the meaning has been lost. To gird means to "summon one's inner resources in preparation for action," or "to prepare yourself mentally to do something difficult."[15] As a military term, it means to "arm, build up, fortify," "get ready for a dangerous situation," or "prepare for a military attack."[16]

This expression originated with the long, flowing robes or tunics worn anciently. A girdle, made of leather or cloth, was often wrapped around the waist. "When men needed freedom to work, run or fight, they would tuck the hem of the tunic into the girdle to gain greater freedom and movement. This action was called 'girding up the loins' and the phrase became a metaphor for preparedness."[17] A contemporary catchphrase would be to "roll up your sleeves."

Girding your loins and *putting on the whole armor of God* are metaphors for our battle with Satan. "The Christian life demands an accurate awareness of a spiritual battle against a strong enemy. . . . His wiles, schemes and tricks are difficult to resist. The Christian soldier must be vigilant and always prepared and ready to do battle for the Lord. . . . [We must] be prepared in every way possible to follow Christ. We are to get rid of every weight and hindrance that would slow us down in our race. We are to take up the cross daily and follow close to Him."[18]

Elder Ballard likened this spiritual preparedness to chain mail, which "consists of dozens of tiny pieces of steel fastened together to allow the user greater flexibility without losing protection. . . . There is not one great and grand thing we can do to arm ourselves spiritually. True spiritual power lies in numerous smaller acts woven together in a fabric of spiritual fortification that protects and shields from all evil."[19] These tiny pieces of metal include the personal and family rituals performed regularly within our homes. "Holy habits"[20] invite the Spirit and provide increased ability to fight the adversary.

Spiritual armor cannot be created in a single moment. It is the culmination of continuous wholesome choices. Christ taught this concept in the parable of the ten virgins. Just as the wise virgins could not share their oil, spiritual shields cannot be given, traded, donated, transferred, bestowed, or bequeathed. Each uniform is individually tailored as a result of personal righteousness.

"Casual commandment keeping"[21] is not enough. Mediocre compliance and "lukewarm commitment weaken faith."[22] Spiritual strength, on the other hand, comes from complete consecration to our covenants. The discipline gained from daily obedience builds strong gospel armor, which is absolutely critical for survival in a world besieged by spiritual assassins. Because life is a battle, our young soldiers are better protected when the whole armor of God is worn all day, *every* day.

When the nearly naked Lamanites battled the well-armored Nephites, they were at greater risk. "And the work of death commenced on both sides, but it was more dreadful on the part of the Lamanites, for their nakedness was exposed to the heavy blows of the Nephites with their swords and their cimeters, which brought death almost at every stroke" (Alma 43:37). When properly worn, gospel regalia provides increased peace, power, and protection for our vulnerable young warriors and is the only real defense against wickedness. Surely Satan trembles when he sees a father and mother faithfully fashioning armor for their children.

Family Boot Camps

In addition to protective body armor, we must implement a rigorous training program for our new recruits. Of necessity, boot camp is difficult and demanding. You cannot make a soldier fit by being soft. Speaking of his experience at boot camp, President Thomas S. Monson said, "For the first three weeks I was convinced my life was in jeopardy. The navy wasn't trying to train me; it was trying to kill me."[23] Nevertheless, daily drills tighten and tone muscles and increase strength and stamina. Likewise, religious drills are basic training for the troops under our tutelage. Turning latter-day soldiers into saints requires repetition. Our family boot camps should increase *spiritual* strength and stamina and tighten and tone testimonies.

While there are many things we can do to fortify our fortresses and the soldiers under our stewardship, this book focuses on five strategies—family prayer, family scripture study, family meals, family home evening, and family traditions. None of these topics are new. They are age-old practices that have been taught by prophets for generations. Mostly, this is a gentle reminder of that which we already know but sometimes forget to implement in our daily routines.

I know all too well that organizing the troops for daily drills can be extremely draining and discouraging. Being drill sergeant for the precious progenies in our platoons is not an enviable position, especially when there's mutiny in the ranks. So why bother? Because we know it is easier to keep up than catch up, and that doing these small and simple things—even when they don't seem small and simple—will keep our soldiers spiritually fit and ready for battle. Regular spiritual repairs and maintenance keep the weeds and dirt and clutter out of our spiritual lives; and brick by brick, day by day, "by small and simple things are great things brought to pass" (Alma 37:6).

Notes

1. M. Russell Ballard, "Like a Flame Unquenchable," *Ensign*, May 1999.

2. M. Russell Ballard, "Be Strong in the Lord," *Ensign*, July 2004.

3. M. Russell Ballard, "The Lord Needs You Now!" *Ensign*, September 2015, 26, 28, 31.

4. Russell M. Nelson, "The Sabbath Is a Delight," *Ensign*, May 2015, 13.

5. Sheri Dew, "Are We Not All Mothers?" *Ensign*, November 2001.

6. Dallin H. Oaks, "Good, Better, Best," *Ensign*, November 2007.

7. L. Tom Perry, "Finding Lasting Peace and Building Eternal Families," *Ensign*, November 2014, 44–45.

8. Julie B. Beck, "Mothers Who Know," *Ensign*, November 2007.

9. Josh Billings, *Goodreads*, accessed October 2015, http://www.goodreads.com/quotes/22649-to-bring-up-a-child-in-the-way-he-should.

10. Gene R. Cook, *Raising Up a Family to the Lord* (Salt Lake City: Deseret Book, 1993), 1.

11. Gary E. Stevenson, "Sacred Homes, Sacred Temples," *Ensign*, May 2009.

12. M. Russell Ballard, "Like a Flame Unquenchable."

13. Linda S. Reeves, "Worthy of Our Promised Blessings," *Ensign*, November 2015, 10.

14. M. Russell Ballard, "Be Strong in the Lord."

15. "Gird loins," *The Free Dictionary*, accessed October 2015, http://idioms.thefreedictionary.com/gird+loins.

16. See "Gird," *Vocabulary*, accessed October 2015, http://www.vocabulary.com/dictionary/gird.

17. Terry Price, "Gird Up Your Loins," Marantha Baptist Seminary, posted September 2007, http://www.mbu.edu/seminary/sunesis/gird-up-your-loins/.

18. Ibid.

19. M. Russell Ballard, "Be Strong in the Lord."

20. Becky Edwards, "Are you putting on the full armor of God every day? Holy habits are the key," *Purpose Driven Motherhood*, posted January 7, 2015, http://purposedrivenmotherhood.blogspot.com/2015/01/are-you-putting-on-full-armor-of-god.html.

21. Gérald Caussé, "Is It Still Wonderful to You?" *Ensign*, May 2015.

22. Kevin W. Pearson, "Stay by the Tree," *Ensign*, May 2015.

23. Thomas S. Monson, "Dare to Stand Alone," *Ensign*, November 2011.

Family
Prayer

Family Prayer

"Pray in your families unto the Father . . . that your
wives and your children may be blessed."

—3 Nephi 18:21

The nightly prayer ritual at our place goes something like this: "Come for prayer" (in our sweetest
parent voices). . . . "Come . . . for . . . prayer" (not quite as
sweetly now). . . . "COME FOR PRAYER!" (in drill sergeant tone and completely lacking any sweetness). Gradually,
one or two children straggle in, then another, and then another.
Ten minutes later, *almost* everyone has at last assembled, except
the charming child who is habitually late and needs a personal
invitation before realizing that the call included him as well. By
the time we finally kneel to pray, someone is usually mad, sad,
crying, giggling, fighting . . . or still showering.

Furthermore, our children often see this rallying of the
troops as the perfect time to share a story or experience from
earlier in the day. And then someone else shares, and by the
time all the sharing ends, you can be sure that someone will
be mad, sad, crying, giggling, fighting . . . or the phone or
doorbell will suddenly be ringing.

Not long ago, as we knelt in the living room for prayer,

listening to several children recount various events of the day, I suddenly noticed car lights in the driveway. "Hurry and say the prayer!" I shrieked. "Someone is here." A quick, ceiling-bouncing prayer was offered just seconds before the doorbell sounded.

When the children were younger, a common post-prayer editorial (always said in their most self-righteous, tattletale tone) went something like this: "Isaac was smiling," or, "Jarom had his eyes open." In their haste to condemn a comrade, they completely failed to realize that their pious accusations were actually self-incriminating.

While praying for family members one night, five-year-old Melia rattled off everyone's name as quickly as possible, "Please bless Dad, Mom, Trenton, Jadee, Caleb, Camille, Isaac, Jarom, Abram, Levi, and Marissa. . . ." She paused a moment before including a personal request in behalf of her ongoing rivalry: "Bless that Levi won't hurt me, and bless that I won't deserve it."

I must admit, family prayer can at times feel more like preparing for battle than pausing politely to praise and petition higher powers. On nights like this, I take solace in the fact that I'm not alone in this dilemma. I often reflect on a remark made by a father, whose children are now grown, recounting his experience of trying to assemble his less-than-willing children for prayer: "By the time we got everyone there, I sometimes felt more like swearing than praying." Haven't we all felt that way a time or two?!

Suggestions for Success

Clearly, my little crew has not perfected family prayer, but we have learned a few things over the years. First, consistency is crucial. If your children know that your family prays every morning before leaving the fortress and again every evening before pulling up the drawbridge, it is much easier to keep up the habit. In fact, your children may even say things like, "Can we pray? I need to leave," or, "Can we have prayer before I go to bed?" Habits create expectations.

And, yes, we should have family prayer morning and evening. President Spencer W. Kimball stressed this point years ago: "In the past, having family prayer once a day may have been all right. But in the future it will not be enough if we are going to save our families."[1]

Another thing my husband and I have found helpful in our family is to give a little bit of lead time before calling for prayer so the children can finish up any last-minute details or tasks. Some of our children like to make their beds and get dressed in the morning before leaving their bedrooms. If we say, "Five minutes to prayer," they can choose to lie in bed for five more minutes or get up, get dressed, and make their beds. Or in the evening, they know they have five minutes to complete a math problem, come to a good stopping place in an essay . . . or finish their shower.

Even with a five-minute warning, they do not always come when called. Years ago, my husband came up with a simple solution to the constant calling and coercing. In a voice loud enough for everyone to hear, he says, "Last one down . . ." Everyone knows that the last one kneeling gets to pray. It works great. The only downside to this method is the chaos and confusion it creates as all the children come spilling out of bedrooms or racing from various places in the house, vying for positions in the prayer circle. It took our daughter-in-law one time to catch on to our gathering-the-family-for-prayer technique. Since then, she is one of the first to kneel. This call-to-arms approach can be a bit treacherous, but, luckily, no one has been seriously injured . . . yet.

A more peaceful—and less dangerous approach—for gathering youngsters is used by the parents of a young family as they softly sing, "Let us gather in a circle and kneel in family prayer."[2] This simple tune creates a reverent mood and prepares their children to pray. I wish we would have thought of this when our children were younger. Another family has each person say one thing they are grateful for before praying. This reminds them of their many blessings and helps them have an attitude of gratitude.

The Power of Prayer

A prominent American judge was once asked what we could do to reduce crime and bring peace to our lives and our nation. The judge said simply, "I would suggest a return to the old-fashioned practice of family prayer."[3] Of all the public programs the judge could have included for changing the culture of our country, I find it intriguing that he suggested something as personal as prayer. "A nation at prayer is a nation at peace."[4]

President Gordon B. Hinckley also suggested "a return to the old pattern of prayer":

> Family prayer in the homes of the people is one of the basic medications that would check the dread disease that is eroding the character of our society. . . .

A generation or two ago, family prayer in the homes of Christian people throughout the world was as much a part of the day's activity as was eating. As that practice has diminished, the moral decay discussed by the Apostle Paul has ensued.

I feel satisfied that there is no adequate substitute for the morning and evening practice of kneeling together—father, mother, and children. This, more than soft carpets, more than lovely draperies, more than cleverly balanced color schemes, is the thing that will make for better and more beautiful homes. . . .

I give you my testimony that if you sincerely apply family prayer, you will not go away unrewarded. The changes may not be readily apparent. They may be extremely subtle. But they will be real, for God "is a rewarder of them that diligently seek him" (Hebrews 11:6).[5]

Family prayers are especially important to those sons and daughters who are on missions, in the military, away at school, or off to camp for a few days. It is comforting to know that their family pleads daily for their protection. My own family has even had prayer with our missionary children at the end of their Mother's Day and Christmas phone calls. Across continents and foreign countries, the Spirit can be felt, and our missionaries have told us that it makes hanging up and the lonely time that follows a little easier to handle.

Often when my family kneels to pray, we remind the person who will be voicing it to remember family, friends, and neighbors who need special blessings. Seeking heaven's help on behalf of others is a tender act, and listening to family members pray for each other is a humbling experience. And sometimes, through the things we say in family prayer, we can affect a child who may not otherwise be persuaded to change.

Prayer opens the way for greater heavenly influence in all aspects of our lives. That is why Amulek encouraged the Zoramites to pray over their flocks, their crops, their households, and their enemies—and for power over the devil (see Alma 34:20–24). He exhorted them to "be watchful unto prayer continually, that ye may not be led away by the temptations of the devil, that he may not overpower you, that ye may not become his subjects at the last day; for behold, he rewardeth you no good thing" (Alma 34:39).

Teach Your Little Ones

Family prayer takes time, but it is worth the effort. The day after President Gordon B. Hinckley's death, seven-year-old Melia prayed sweetly, "And bless that President Hinckley will have a good time in heaven. And bless that he will be happy. And bless that the new prophet will do a good job."

Before our grandson Eli could even talk, he would drop to his knees, arms folded and head bowed, the instant anyone called for family prayer. His little sister, Eden, delicately places one hand on top of the other when it's time to pray. And our daughter's two sons, Mason and Carter, are quick to give kisses to everyone in the circle as soon as the prayer has ended. It is comforting to know that our grandchildren are being well taught.

One evening, however, three-year-old Mason was reluctant to pray. Gently coaching him, my daughter suggested, "Just say what is in your heart." This seemed simple enough, and he did exactly as his mother instructed. Head bowed, he stated reverently, "The blood in my heart is pumping, pumping, pumping." Another time, he mumbled through the entire family prayer his father offered. Afterward, my daughter decided he needed a few tips on appropriate behavior during prayer: bow your head, fold your arms, close your eyes, and *don't talk.* "But Papa was talking!" the little guy protested.

The benefits of family prayer far exceed any inconvenience we may encounter along the way. Praying as a family builds unity and invites the Spirit into our homes. Through this process, we teach our children that God is real and that He hears and answers prayers. That is one of the most precious things a child can know. Then, when they are faced with their own perplexing problems, they will know where to turn for help. The moment of crisis is not the time to be desperately fashioning spiritual armor.

Fasting and Prayer

Sometimes, however, prayer alone is not enough. Receiving increased heavenly aid may require fervent prayer coupled with fasting. When Christ's Apostles wondered why they could not cast the devil out of a man, the Savior chastised them, "Howbeit this kind goeth not out but by prayer *and* fasting" (Matthew 17:21; emphasis added). The sons of Mosiah were successful in their missions to convert the Lamanites in large part because "they fasted much and prayed much that the Lord would grant unto them a portion of his Spirit to go with them" (Alma 17:9). Alma also "fasted and prayed many days" that he might know the things of God (Alma 5:46). And when the Nephites desired to come closer to God, they "did fast and pray oft, and did wax stronger and stronger in their humility, and firmer and firmer in the faith of Christ, unto the filling their souls with joy" (Helaman 3:35).

Long ago, the prophet Isaiah outlined the great blessings associated with the law of the fast:

> To loose the bands of wickedness, to undo the heavy burdens, and to let the oppressed go free, and that ye break every yoke. . . .
>
> Then shall thy light break forth as the morning, and thine health shall spring forth speedily: and thy righteousness shall go before thee; the glory of the Lord shall be thy rereward.
>
> Then shalt thou call, and the Lord shall answer; thou shalt cry, and he shall say, Here I am . . . then shall thy light rise in obscurity, and thy darkness be as the noonday:
>
> And the Lord shall guide thee continually, and satisfy thy soul in drought, and make fat thy bones: and thou shalt be like a watered garden, and like a spring of water, whose waters fail not. (Isaiah 58:6, 8–11)

Those are powerful promises! Fasting works. I am a personal witness to the miracles that can happen. Family fasts combined with prayer are wonderful ways to strengthen your family's spiritual armor.

In our family, we offer two special family prayers in connection with fast day—one at the beginning and one at the end. When the children first began fasting, they had a tendency to eat until bedtime and resume as soon as we came home from church. Eventually, we started having family prayer after the last meal on Saturday (signaling the start of the fast) and again just before dinner on Sunday (signaling the end). We also encourage them to begin and end their fasts with personal prayer. This has eliminated the snacking and helped them maintain a more complete fast.

Grudgingly going without sustenance is simply starving; willingly abstaining with a prayer and a purpose is fasting. When God knows that something is so important that you are willing to go without eating and drinking to get it, He takes notice. Fasting and prayer are an impressive duo for obtaining marvelous blessings, and helping your children live the law of the fast will benefit their lives immeasurably.

An important aspect of a monthly fast includes an offering to the poor. There is a direct correlation between our payments and our prayers. "One of the important things the Lord has told us to do is to be liberal in our payment of fast offerings," President Marion G. Romney taught. "I would like you to know that there are great rewards for so doing—both spiritual and temporal rewards. The Lord says that the efficacy of our prayers depends upon our liberality to the poor."[6] Don't shortchange yourself by being stingy with the Lord.

Prayer Is Work

Not only does our generosity affect our prayers, but we must also be careful that our petitions to the Lord are sincere and in harmony with His will. Mormon warned that if we pray without "real intent of heart . . . it profiteth [us] nothing, for God receiveth none such" (Moroni 7:9). The Bible Dictionary defines prayer as "the act by which the will of the Father and the will of the child are brought into correspondence with each other. The object of prayer is not to change the will of God but to secure for ourselves and for others blessings that God is already willing to grant but that are made conditional on our asking for them. Blessings require some work or effort on our part before we can obtain them. Prayer is a form of work and is an appointed means for obtaining the highest of all blessings" (Bible Dictionary, "Prayer"). Is it possible that there are blessings your family is missing out on simply because you have not asked, and are you willing to put forth the necessary effort to obtain them?

God is aware of us. He knows the desires of our hearts and wants to be involved in the intimate and important details of our lives. But He also wants us to do our part. When Alma sought divine guidance, he "inquired diligently" (Alma 40:3, 9) and "labored much in the spirit, wrestling with God in mighty prayer" (Alma 8:10). Enos "hungered . . . before [his] Maker, and . . . cried unto him in mighty prayer . . . all the day long . . . and . . . prayed unto him with many long strugglings. . . . And it came to pass that after [he] had prayed and labored with all diligence . . . [and] cried unto him continually," the Lord *finally* answered (Enos 1:4, 11–12, 15). And when the brother of Jared sought help for his friends and family, he "did cry unto the Lord, and the Lord had compassion" (Ether 1:37). A careful review of this story reveals that the brother of Jared did not just cry once—he cried *repeatedly* unto the Lord. I wonder if there is a connection between the consistency of our cries and the Lord's compassion. Some prayers take time, but whether they are answered sooner or later, every earnest prayer reaches heaven's portals—of that I am certain.

Daily Prayer Is Important

There is great power in prayer, and Satan knows it. It is the first line of defense against his diabolical schemes, and he will do anything he can to prevent it. He knows that when your family has a relationship with Father in Heaven—his archenemy—his power is greatly diminished. Do not give in to Satan's attempts to thwart family prayer. "Which parent in Book of Mormon times would have let their sons march out to the front of battle without a breastplate and shield and sword to protect them against the potentially mortal blows of the enemy? But how many of us let our children march out the front door each morning to the most dangerous of all battlefields, to face Satan and his myriad temptations, without their spiritual [armor] that [comes] from the protective power of prayer?"[7]

Pausing daily to invoke heaven's blessings on our homes and households is a small and simple thing, but brick by brick, this daily drill strengthens our stripling warriors and brings blessings to our families, our communities, and our nation. "Pray [in your families] always, that you may come off conqueror" (D&C 10:5). "Family prayer should be a non-negotiable priority in your daily life."[8]

Notes

1. Spencer W. Kimball, as quoted by James E. Faust, "Teaching Children Through Example and Instruction," *Marriage and Family Relations, Participant's Study Guide* (Salt Lake City: Intellectual Reserve, 2000), 49.

2. DeVota Mifflin Peterson, "Family Prayer," *Children's Songbook* (Salt Lake City: Deseret Book, 1991), 189.

3. Thomas S. Monson, "Come unto Him in Prayer and Faith," *Ensign*, March 2009.

4. Gordon B. Hinckley, "Family Prayer, Family Scripture Study, and Family Home Evening," *Marriage and Family Relations, Participant's Study Guide*, 69.

5. Ibid.

6. *Book of Mormon Student Manual, Religion 121 and 122*, chapter 44 (Salt Lake City: Intellectual Reserve, 1996), 125.

7. Tad R. Callister, "Parents: The Prime Gospel Teachers of Their Children," *Ensign,* November 2014, 33.

8. Richard G. Scott, "Make the Exercise of Faith Your First Priority," *Ensign*, November 2014, 93.

Prayer

Family Scripture Study

Family Scripture Study

"For my soul delighteth in the scriptures,
and my heart pondereth them."

—2 Nephi 4:15

I wish I could say that it's always perfect," lamented one young mother, "but it's not. Sometimes someone needs an emergency bathroom break, or someone steals someone else's book, or someone reads a word wrong and someone else giggles and then someone starts to cry, or someone won't be quiet or sit still or stop burping in someone's face . . . or the kids start to fight over who gets the couch, and then mom and dad yell and *whoosh*! The good feeling is gone. We've had our fair share of times like that. But the longer we keep trying over and over again to make it work, the better it gets."[1]

Even when it isn't perfect, family scripture time can still have an impact. "Come to scripture study so you can feel the Spirit in your heart," seven-year-old Marissa coaxed her brothers when they delayed. And when my husband was reading the story of King Noah and Abinadi to the children before bed years ago, my young son bemoaned what seemed his inevitable fate: "When I grow up and get burned in a fire, I'll be sad." Don't underestimate children's listening and learning abilities, even though young and restless and wiggly and disengaged. They are probably taking in more than you realize.

I must confess, in the hustle and bustle of our family's life, daily scripture reading has, at times, been a bit sporadic. While reading the Book of Mormon a few years ago, we came to the part where Nephi was on the tower praying for the people (Helaman 7). Several days passed without reading, so my husband started out by bringing us up to speed on where we had last ended: "Okay now, Nephi is on the tower praying—" but before he could finish, Jarom exclaimed, "Still?! He's been up there all week." It was a painful reminder of our slacking.

The ever-constant goal is to have family scripture time right before evening prayer, but sometimes there is a vast chasm between resolve and reality. Years ago, we tried doing it in the morning with a short family devotional, but the older the children grew, the more difficult it became. Then our oldest son got a job that required him to leave at 5:40 a.m., and getting the children out of bed at that hour would have been impossible.

Regardless of when my family tries it, one thing is almost certain: someone will be mad, sad, crying, giggling, fighting . . . or sleeping. Sometimes the children just stare blankly into space, completely unaware of the important doctrine we are trying to distill upon them. The little darlings get so easily distracted, and sometimes we have wondered whether it was even worth it. But in spite of the seemingly insignificant transformation, over time, we have seen that regular doses of family scripture reading absolutely do make a difference.

Suggestions for Scripture Study

One young mother gives several suggestions for making this daily event go more smoothly:

1. Find a Good Spot! I believe finding a regular place for family scripture study helps everyone to participate and be a little more reverent. For our family, we try to read in our formal living room. . . . [as] it lacks many of the distractions of the rest of our house like toys, television, even food! . . . Even our smallest toddlers know that we are doing something special when we gather as a family to read in the living room. The location is an outward reminder of what is expected from each person.

2. Have a Stack of Scriptures Ready! . . . It might not seem like it at first, but having the books waiting and ready has done wonders for simplifying our family scripture study.

3. Set Reminders on All Electronic Devices! . . . At eight o'clock at night, all of our phones, iPods, iPads, and computers start chirping and dinging with the same reminder: Family Scripture Time! It is hard to ignore, and we promised ourselves that we would heed that reminder no matter what.

4. Give Everyone a Chance to Read! . . . It might be slower going, but it works so much better if everyone gets a chance to participate. . . . Even non-readers can join in. I have always had my littlest ones repeat after me, word for word, when it is their turn. . . . My preschooler started to recognize the phrase, "And it came to pass," all on his own. . . . I might be imagining things, but I have a sneaking suspicion that scripture reading has improved their overall reading.[2]

Another mother offers some additional suggestions:

Skits and stories. We love scripture skits! . . . Being in the story makes it stick. Then of course discuss any lessons you can pull from the story. . . .

Drawing or journaling. Have your kids draw a picture of something your family is reading that day. Or invite them to write about something they learned after reading it. . . .

Read, summarize, principle. . . . Each family member takes a turn reading 4–5 verses, and then summarizes what he or she just read. Summarizing makes you think! Then the person finds a principle, which is a truth you can use. One way to find a principle is to ask, "What's a life lesson in this passage?" . . . You can also ask each family member to share their favorite take-away or life lesson from today's reading, and/or set a goal of how to apply what you learned.

Read on their own and discuss together. Family members do their reading on their own . . . and then the family gets together to discuss what they read. Perhaps each person could read aloud his or her favorite verse from the given chapter and share why [they] liked it. . . .

Scripture party! You could set a goal to read the whole Book of Mormon and then . . . throw a party to celebrate when you finish.

Double up with Church programs. Sometimes we read the scripture verses required to pass off a goal in a child's Personal Progress, Faith in God, or Duty to God program, and then discuss them together as a family.

Make it a devotional. In our family we spend a little extra time adding a few things to our scripture study. . . . We have one person conduct . . . welcoming the family and asking for that day's announcements. That person gets to choose someone to pick a song . . . and someone to say a family prayer. We review a quote or verse we're memorizing, and then that person can choose how we're going to study our scriptures that day.

Testify. . . . It might sound awkward to bear testimony in your own family room with your own family. It doesn't need to be! I do it often informally. I might say, "I testify that what Alma just said about Christ's Atonement is true. Christ really did die for us and suffer for all our challenges and sins. I don't know how I could go through life without knowing that." . . .

As you testify and invite others to testify you are inviting the Spirit to come in and confirm the truth to everyone in the room. Be sure to explain once in a while what your kids are feeling so they know how to recognize the Spirit. "Wow, I feel the Spirit about what we just read. It makes me feel peaceful and good inside. That's the Holy Ghost telling me it's true. Have you ever felt that feeling when we're reading the scriptures?" Your enthusiasm and love for the scriptures is contagious, so let it show by how you talk about them.[3]

I second what these two mothers have said. Reading the scriptures together promotes greater faith and unity, bringing us closer to each other and to the Lord. It also "promotes the sharing of values between generations" and "provides the opportunity for testimonies to be gained and borne"; it "creates a family worship time" and "a daily focus on God, others, and self, thus bringing about repentance and a desire to change"; and it "allows time for loving, sharing, understanding, and listening" and "gives children an opportunity to raise some of the concerns they face in school or with their peers and then to have those items discussed by the family and related to the words of the Lord."[4] The scriptures also contain wonderful, righteous heroes for children to emulate. No wonder one family calls scripture reading their daily spoonful of sugar. It is the little bit of sweetness that helps counteract all that is bitter in the world.

Despite my own family's sometimes inadequate daily dose of scripture reading, one thing we have done consistently since our children were young is to have an extended scripture study on the Sabbath day. After all, one of the reasons for the revised Sunday block schedule was for parents to have more time to teach their children. These sessions last anywhere from half an hour to an hour and a half, depending on comments and concerns generated by family members. We stop frequently to ask questions, offer opinions, and discuss passages.

Snorkeling, Scuba Diving, and Feasting

Like the layers of an onion, the scriptures have multiple meanings. Do not just peel back the first one and feel satisfied that you have learned enough. There is a difference between skimming and searching the scriptures, just as there is a difference between snorkeling and scuba diving. One is a casual surface activity and the other is complete immersion. Both experiences are enjoyable, but one is more compelling. Don't be afraid to jump in with both feet.

The scriptures counsel us all to "feast upon the words of Christ" (2 Nephi 32:3) and "let your soul delight in fatness" (2 Nephi 9:51). *Feasting* implies far more than occasional snacking or tentative nibbling. The scriptures are not fast food or grab-and-go meals. They are a smorgasbord of gospel insights and information. They are the words of life—eternal life. They contain the principles and doctrines that, when understood and followed, will exalt your family. Daily dining at this spiritual buffet will not only nourish but will also fill your family's hungry souls. Make them a delicious part of your day.

Personal Scripture Time

On a personal note, I learned the value of scripture reading shortly after the birth of my sixth child. Up to this point, I had managed to carve out personal study time in and around dishes, diapering, laundry, cooking, cleaning, and caring for little ones. However, this newest baby seemed to leave no spare time at all. As the days wore on, I rationalized that mothering was every bit as important as studying. Surely, God could see how incredibly busy I was and would understand. . . .

Then one day, I had a troubling thought. What if God did not understand, and what if He did not excuse me? Then and there, I decided I had better change my approach. In an effort to squeeze more time into my daily schedule for this important task, I finally settled on an efficient *read-and-feed* strategy—every time I sat down to feed the baby, I took my scriptures with me. Suddenly, I had plenty of scripture time.

This was an important pivot point for me, and I learned several things. First, I *desperately* need those few minutes every day to step out of the world and into eternity. With all the stress of family life, I need a chance to reflect, refocus, and regroup. I need time to ponder those things that matter most. This personal introspection gives me a chance to analyze my life and how well it aligns with God's will. It also puts the never-ending grind of motherhood into proper perspective.

During these daily devotionals, I have learned to love the scriptures. They are priceless, cherished moments.

Second, the scriptures were written for me. They provide a pattern for life. I don't have to blindly make my way, learning everything firsthand. By reading the stories of others and how they faced their own personal battles, I have learned crucial strategies for conquering my own challenges.

Third, knowing gospel truths has greatly helped me in my mothering. Because of my daily studies, I have often been able to answer my children's questions with specific scripture references, examples, and stories. This has been a great blessing. God needs latter-day mother-generals who understand doctrine and can teach it to their children.

Expound and Explore

Become a student of the scriptures and help your family members become students as well. Take it slow. Expound and explore. Look for lessons to be learned. "You ought not to read for mileage."[5] Scripture reading should not be one more detail in a long to-do list. It is at the heart of our parenting responsibilities. There is no set number of pages or passages we must read each day. When we read for mileage, we miss important teaching opportunities with our children. But when we take the time to dissect and discuss the scriptures, they will become much more than holy history books of faraway places and forgotten peoples. They will become convincingly real and will provide practical approaches and proven strategies for enduring our own tests and trials.

For example, instead of merely reading the story of Abinadi

getting burned by fire as an unfortunate incident, we could ask ourselves, "What would *we* do if a teacher or a friend or an employer threatened *us* because of our beliefs? Would *we* be willing to stand firm in our beliefs and endure persecution, ridicule, or even death?" Or, while reading the story of Lehi, we could ask ourselves, "Would *we* be willing to give up nearly all of our worldly possessions to go on an eight-year trek through the wilderness—eating raw meat and giving birth in a tent? Would *we* have been an obedient Nephi or a murmuring Laman or Lemuel?" We could also consider the fact that while we may not be asked to permanently leave our homes, young men and senior couples have been asked to temporarily leave to serve missions. In contrast to Lehi and Sariah's experience, a one- or two-year mission seems like a rather reasonable sacrifice.

In addition to not passing quickly over scripture stories, don't simply skip over words or phrases that are unfamiliar. Increased clarity and understanding can often be found in the footnotes, cross references, or Bible Dictionary. Have you taken time to discuss the difference between *strait* and *straight*, or how the meaning of Alma's teaching on planting a seed in our hearts would change if *word* were capitalized (see Alma 32 and John 1:1)? Recently, while reading as a family, our son asked what *encumbrances* meant, and we spent several minutes on a scriptural detour, helping him find an answer.

Sunday Scripture Study

Scripture reading can be extremely rewarding. We have had marvelous chats with our children on Sunday afternoons while marking, searching, and discussing the scriptures. Some of our best lessons and most effective teaching moments have occurred spontaneously during family study time.

When we first began these longer study sessions, we took turns reading by moving in circular fashion from one person to another, each person reading two verses at a time. However, it did not take long for some of the children to figure out that by counting ahead, they could calculate which verses they would read next and catch a quick nap before it was their turn again. This problem was easily remedied by doing popcorn reading—one person reads one to four verses and then calls on anyone in the room to read. You never know who will be called on next, and you never know where the reader will end. Our children sometimes make it even more interesting by reading only half of a verse or half of a sentence. No more daydreaming with this method!

In the days of babies and toddlers, I found it helpful to make sure they were fed and diapered before launching into lengthy gospel discussions. I also found that the littlest ones were less distracting if they colored quietly or played nearby while the rest of us read. As they grew, their desire to participate increased, so we purchased inexpensive paperback scriptures for them. At age eight, they received their own set of scriptures. By this age, they could read well enough to follow along while others read; and by reading with the family, they learned to pronounce and understand the language of the scriptures. When they went on their missions, their scriptures were marked and ready to use.

In addition to reading directly from the scriptures, we often read to the littlest ones from the illustrated scripture stories produced by the Church. The abundance of pictures kept their interest and the wording was easily understood. I also used them as beginning readers for my young children. They mastered reading skills while learning gospel principles. To this day, our children will sometimes comment on a picture from those books when recounting scripture stories.

And, just to mix things up a little, we occasionally play scripture trivia. Before we were married, my husband acquired two sets of LDS game cards—*Seek* and *Zion*. You may be able to find these in used bookstores or at Deseret Industries. This is a fun way to test our knowledge of scripture details and have a lively dialogue on a variety of gospel topics. And sometimes we play scripture *Pictionary* or scripture charades. The children enjoy the occasional diversions.

Don't be afraid to dive deep into gospel topics with your children. You don't need to be a scriptorian to teach from the scriptures. More than once, a child's question has sent us scurrying to our home library to research the answer. It is perfectly acceptable to admit you don't know but are willing to find out, and it is fun to learn together.

Use the Scriptures to Make Family Rules

"Teach the word of the Lord diligently unto your children, not just in formal settings but . . . 'when thou sittest in thine house, and when thou walkest by the way, and when thou liest down, and when thou risest up.'"[6] Refer to the scriptures often. Use them to resolve family issues and "to be the source of family rules."[7] Paul taught that "all scripture is given by inspiration of God, and is profitable for doctrine, for reproof, for correction, for instruction in righteousness" (2 Timothy 3:16). And Nephi counseled us to "liken all scriptures unto us, that it might be for our profit and learning" (1 Nephi 19:23). After all, it is not "about just reading the scriptures but rather about adopting His words to govern your life so that they become the standard works—the standard for your works."[8]

How many times have you said in frustration, "Why don't these children come with an instruction manual?!" Actually, they do. The best parenting books were given by God Himself. Within the pages of His holy writ are critical strategies for countering Satan's charades and helping families lead happy, productive lives that are in harmony with His will. They are the most important books you can read on rearing children and raising them in righteousness. "When your children have a problem, do your best to read a passage from the scriptures to give them direction from the Lord. Not only will the counsel be correct but it will also teach your children to rely upon the scriptures in obtaining answers to their problems."[9]

Elder Gene R. Cook told the story of his teenage daughters feeling pressure to dress like their peers. As they read Isaiah's comments on the dress standards of the women of the last days (see 2 Nephi 13:18–23), he and his wife had an opportunity to bear testimony of the principles they were reading, and their daughters began asking questions.

> As [they] worked through those questions . . . a standard evolved about what the Lord expects of a righteous young woman in properly adorning herself. The standard was not [their] standard, but it was based on a standard given in the

scriptures. In other words, it was the Lord's standard. . . . Thus, they accepted it as their own and lived it from that day forward. . . . What made this experience so powerful was the fact that had it been just [their] standard, [they] would later have had to enforce it with more specific rules and perhaps . . . discuss it frequently with [their] children.[10]

I also had an interesting scripture-mentoring moment with one of my daughters. The day after a high school football game, she chattered excitedly about the previous evening, describing in great detail the events that had transpired. The more she talked, the more concerned I became. Her behavior had not been sinful or dangerous, but it was quite out of character and not exemplary of a latter-day young woman.

Later, when we were alone, I gently reminded her that, as a covenant daughter of God, she had promised to stand as a witness "at all times and in all things, and in all places" (Mosiah 18:9)—even at a football game. I told her that someone was always watching and that her behavior *always* mattered. The next day, I received a nice hand-written note. In addition to expressing kind words of love and gratitude, she thanked me for bringing her inappropriate behavior to her attention and for "certain phrases that struck home."

Even if your children don't follow your counsel or the counsel that is given in the scriptures, never give up. When they start getting their personal questions answered from the scriptures, they will begin to see their value and learn to appreciate them. Then scripture reading will no longer be such a chore.

The Power of the Word

There is power in the word of God. As Helaman taught, "Whosoever will may lay hold upon the word of God, which is quick and powerful, which shall divide asunder all the cunning and the snares and the wiles of the devil, and lead the man of Christ in a strait and narrow course across that everlasting gulf of misery which is prepared to engulf the wicked" (Helaman 3:29).

Elder M. Russell Ballard also explained,

> When Nephi's brothers asked him what the meaning of the rod of iron was, Nephi "said unto them that it was the word of God; and whoso would hearken unto the word of God, and would hold fast unto it, they would never perish; neither could the temptations and the fiery darts of the adversary overpower them unto blindness, to lead them away to destruction" (1 Nephi 15:24).
>
> Isn't that the protective power that we all seek? . . . Note the choice of verbs Nephi used. . . . He said that we must "hearken" . . . and "hold fast." . . . This implies much more than a cursory, occasional reading. . . . We must . . . cling to those principles as though our very lives depended on it—which, if we are speaking of spiritual life, is literally true.[11]

"If you want your children to recognize, understand, and act on the promptings of the Spirit," warns Elder Richard G. Scott, "you must study the scriptures with them. Don't yield to Satan's lie that you don't have time to study the scriptures. . . . Feasting on the word of God each day is more important than sleep, school, work, television shows, video games, or social media. You may need to reorganize your priorities to provide time for the study of the word of God."[12]

Years ago, President Ezra Taft Benson made a promise regarding religious instruction in the home: "Take time daily to read the scriptures together as a family. Individual scripture reading is important, but *family scripture reading is vital*. Reading the Book of Mormon together as a family will especially bring increased spirituality into your home and will give both parents and children the power to resist temptation and to have the Holy Ghost as their constant companion. I promise you that the Book of Mormon will change the lives of your family."[13]

What parent would not want increased spirituality in their home and increased power to resist temptation? I add my testimony to President Benson's. Our family study sessions have given our young soldiers a strong scriptural foundation. It has also instilled in them a desire for personal scripture time, and I regularly find them in solitary places studying on their own. Scripture reading may seem like a small and simple thing, but brick by brick it has made a dramatic difference in our family. It is, without a doubt, one of the most profound things we have done with our children.

Notes

1. Rindi Jacobsen, "5 Tips for Successful Family Scripture Study with Young Children," *The Jacobsens*, posted November 25, 2014, gregandrindi.blogspot.com.

2. Ibid.

3. Becky Edwards, "Scripture Feasting Tool #6—Kids! 11 Fun Ideas to Get Your Kids in the Scriptures," *Purpose Driven Motherhood*, posted July 5, 2015, http://purposedrivenmotherhood.blogspot .com/2015/07/scripture-feasting-tool-6-kids-eleven.html.

4. Gene R. Cook, *Raising Up a Family to the Lord* (Salt Lake City: Deseret Book, 1993), 114.

5. Ibid., 119–20.

6. Ibid., 22.

7. Janet Foster, personal correspondence.

8. Lawrence E. Corbridge, "The Most Important Things," *Ensign*, February 2015, 71.

9. Gene R. Cook, *Raising Up a Family to the Lord*.

10. Ibid.

11. M. Russell Ballard, "Be Strong in the Lord," *Ensign*, July 2004.

12. Richard G. Scott, "Make the Exercise of Faith Your First Priority," *Ensign*, November 2014, 93.

13. Ezra Taft Benson, "To the Mothers in Zion" (a fireside for parents, February 22, 1987); emphasis added.

Prayer ~~ Scripture Study

Family Meals

Family Meals

"Better is a dinner of herbs where love is,
than a stalled ox and hatred therewith."

—Proverbs 15:17

$\mathcal{S}$itting with her family at the dinner table discussing the day's events, six-year-old Adelyn announced, "You know what the best parts of the day are? They are breakfast and dinner because the whole family is together."[1]

Sadly, the notion of a family sharing a meal is something of a Norman Rockwell illustration from a bygone era. In today's hurried and harried have-it-now world, the quintessential quiet family gathering around the dinner table has been replaced with dine-in, carry-out, fast food, and premade toss-it-in-the-microwave meals; and many parents wonder if it really matters if everyone does it at the same time. The primary purpose of mealtimes has been minimized to filling bellies—on our way to other "more important" things—not nourishing inner needs. But what if the meal *is* the most important thing? And what if how we eat it is actually more important than what we eat?

Listening to a commercial on the radio recently, I heard

them refer to the dinner table as the original entertainment center. Eating together is "a ritual that was virtually universal a generation ago but has undergone a striking transformation. No longer honored by society as a time of day that must be set aside, some families see family supper as little more than a quaint relic. But others are beginning to recognize it as a lifeline—a way to connect with their loved ones on a regular basis and to get more enjoyment out of family life."[2]

Mealtime Madness

I will be the first to admit that sitting at supper surrounded by a crowd of little and not so little children is not always the most pleasant experience. One night as the family sat waiting for the meal to begin, I proudly placed a pan of lasagna in the center of the table. In an attempt to instill gratitude for my daily efforts, my husband kindly reminded the children that they should be thankful for the nice meals I regularly prepared. My five-year-old daughter gazed thoughtfully at the strange concoction of red tomato sauce and melted cheese abstractly swirled together, then declared dryly, "It looks like throw up."

And, for a *long* time, one of my sons spilled his milk at nearly every meal. One time, he even spilled ketchup all over new kitchen carpet at his grandparent's. Another time when they took some of the children out for pizza, he spilled the entire pitcher of root beer. That ended the eating out with the grandparents! Just the other day, this charming twenty-three-year-old spilled his milk *again*. In an instant, all the spilling of years gone by came back to me. Finally, I could chuckle.

In addition to complaints about the cuisine and plenty

of spilled milk, there have been ample portions of jabbering and jousting, teasing and tattling, and chomping and chasing. It's enough to give me indigestion! There was a point in time when I'd had just about all I could take of this mealtime madness. With a bunch of busy little boys who spent a good part of the meal running around the table or climbing on or under it rather than sitting calmly in their seats like civilized people, I decided something had to be done.

During one meal, my husband and I conspired to act up, demonstrating nearly every form of bad behavior used by the children—laughing loudly, chewing obnoxiously, chasing each other around the table, crawling under it, and reaching over it to grab whatever we needed. Our hope was that by seeing how ridiculous we looked, they would modify their own manners to conform to accepted normal standards of decency. Our older children were dumbfounded, but the little ones were delighted—Mom and Dad were playing their kind of game and seemed to be having a wonderful time. Not to be outdone, Jarom, the frequent instigator of the dinner-time disasters, got a mischievous gleam in his eye and, before we knew it, he and his younger brothers had joined us in the chase around the table. That's when we knew the plan had backfired!

Benefits of Eating Together

Regardless of the chaos that has often accompanied our family's feeding frenzies, research has shown that eating as a family has far-reaching results. It satisfies not only physical needs but emotional ones as well.

This is where the tribe comes to transmit wisdom, embed expectations, confess, conspire, forgive, repair. The idealized version is as close to a regular worship service, with its litanies and lessons and blessings, as a family gets outside a sanctuary. . . .

There is something about a shared meal—not some holiday blowout, not once in a while but regularly, reliably—that anchors a family. . . . And on those evenings when the mood is right and the family lingers . . . you get a glimpse of the power of this habit and why social scientists say such communion acts as a kind of vaccine, protecting kids from all manner of harm.[3]

Studies show that "it's in the teenage years that this daily investment pays some of its biggest dividends. . . . The more often families eat together, the less likely kids are to smoke, drink, do drugs, get depressed, develop eating disorders and consider suicide, and the more likely they are to do well in school."[4] All that protection from something as simple as eating together! Why not give it a try? "If it were just about food, we would squirt it into their mouths with a tube."[5]

Long before this research came out, a prophet of God encouraged mothers "to be together at mealtimes as often as possible."[6] And in recent years, there has been increased counsel from Church leaders to make our meals a primary focus in fortifying families. Every chance he gets, Satan seeks to divide and conquer, to undermine and separate; God seeks to unify and strengthen. Clearly, there is more to mealtime than teasing our taste buds and testing our patience.

In fact, you just might be surprised at the delicious things that can happen during dinner. One evening while dining on parlor pizza—a special treat at our house—Levi meticulously pulled off all the pepperoni on his slice of pizza and placed them in a pile to be eaten at the end of the meal. As he lifted the now sparsely adorned pizza to his mouth, eagerly anticipating the moment, he exclaimed, "Ahhh . . . *pepperoni* pizza!" Then he chomped down with great satisfaction. The entire family erupted into laughter—everyone but Levi, who was too intent on eating to notice the irony. Had we not been at the table together, we would have missed this moment and this memory—one we laugh about often while eating pizza.

President Thomas S. Monson once told the story of Jack McDonnell, a medical doctor and the son of a Methodist minister. Growing up, Jack's family was incredibly poor, but every evening while they sat at dinner, his father would ask each of the seven children, "And what did you do for someone today?"[7] The children, knowing they would be reporting to their father, developed a habit of daily service. This became their "father's most valuable legacy, for *that* expectation and *those* words inspired [Jack] and his siblings to help others throughout their lives."[8] Dr. McConnell went on to create Volunteers in Medicine—free clinics for the uninsured. There are now ninety-six of these clinics in the United States, all because a father used mealtime to make an impact.

Eating Is an Educational Experience

Eating as a family is also an educational experience. Children learn important cooking, cleaning, and communication skills while chopping, mixing, stirring, dicing, chatting, and doing dishes. They learn to listen and respond courteously and to wait for their turn to speak. They learn to try new foods, eat their vegetables, pass the food, and sit politely. "The message embedded in the microwave was that time spent standing in front of a stove was time wasted. But something precious was lost . . . when cooking came to be cast as drudgery and meals as discretionary. . . . It turns out that when kids help prepare a meal, they are much more likely to eat it, and it's a useful skill that seems to build self-esteem."[9]

Mealtime Is Family Time

The benefits of being together at mealtime go far beyond the few minutes spent eating. "Meals together send the message that citizenship in a family entails certain standards beyond individual whims. This is where a family builds its identity and culture. Legends are passed down, jokes rendered, eventually the wider world examined through the lens of a family's values. . . . [It is] worth some inconvenience or compromise to make meals together a priority."[10]

When my son Caleb was twelve, his weekly Scout meeting began an hour before dinner, and the first few times he attended, we started eating before he returned. One day as he left the house, his parting comment to me came in the form of a gentle rebuke: "Don't eat without me." Intuitively, he knew something I had not consciously considered—eating as a family is important. Even a near-teenager, whose sole purpose in life seemed to be consuming as much food as possible as often as possible, did not want to do it alone.

In a *Time* magazine article, Nancy Gibbs wrote,

The older the kids are, the more they may need this protected time together, but the less likely they are to get it. . . . Teens who ate three or fewer meals a week with their families wished they did so more often. Parents sometimes seem a little too eager to be rejected by their teenage sons and daughters. . . . Parents may be undervaluing themselves when they conclude that sending kids off to every conceivable extracurricular activity is a better use of time than an hour spent around a table, just talking to Mom and Dad.[11]

So turn off the TV, the computer, and the phones, and savor some special time with children. With the advent of cell phones, we established *no-phone zones* in our home; mealtime is one of the most important of those zones. Even when my husband served as bishop, we rarely answered the phone during a meal. Eliminating intrusions while eating tells your children they are more important than anything else you could be doing.

Children should also understand that their presence at the family dinner table is expected. This is more likely to happen if they are served at regular times each day so family members can plan their schedules accordingly. When the family is together, try to make it a pleasant experience—laugh, talk, reminisce, tell jokes, and ask questions. Make it something they look forward to. Many times, my family has lingered long after the food has been consumed, chitchatting on a variety of topics. Those are magical moments.

Listen as your children share their embarrassing, awkward, discouraging, rewarding, and humorous stories. You might be surprised at the things you will learn by simply paying attention. Our oldest son regularly had stories to share, and we loved hearing them. One day shortly before he moved out, my youngest daughter declared dismally, "Now we aren't going to hear Trenton's stories anymore." I must admit, the table seemed a little lonely without him.

A friend's family uses dinnertime to discuss current events or to tell one incident of awesomeness they experienced that day. You could also play the "bad & good" game—each family member sharing one positive and one negative aspect of their day. "Research has found that by watching others (including Mom and Dad) navigate ups and downs in real time, children develop empathy and solidarity with those around them."[12]

Meaningful and Memorable Mealtimes

The bottom line is to make your mealtimes meaningful and memorable. In addition to having fun, powerful lessons can be taught while surrounding the kitchen table. Years ago, we ate a meal blindfolded. After, we had a lesson on what it would be like to be blind and being grateful for our blessings. Inviting neighbors and nonmembers to dinner is a casual way to become acquainted and have religious discussions. We have had many missionary moments sharing meals with friends.

But not all of our meals have included a table. Some of our favorite mealtime memories have been made on a blanket under the shade of a tree in the backyard. It's amazing how much better peanut butter sandwiches and Kool-Aid taste when eaten outside on a warm, sunny day with a gentle breeze.

Birthday meals at our house are also special. The day begins with our traditional birthday breakfast: grits, eggs, and bacon or sausage. For dinner, the guest of honor gets to choose the menu and eat off the "birthday plate"—a colorful plate reserved for this occasion. It includes a cheery reminder of just how much they are loved: "This big day comes just once a year; hip hip hooray! Your birthday's here! We all love you; we think you're great. . . . And now, c'mon, let's celebrate! Happy birthday!"

For me, holiday meals are a lot more fun with festive table centerpieces, colored napkins, and food that commemorates the occasion. Even breakfast can be special—colored oatmeal, colored milk (don't forget to drop in a spider on Halloween), or colored pancakes in shapes to match the holiday—hearts, shamrocks, bunnies, jack-o'-lanterns, and Christmas trees. I have also used cookie cutters to press holiday shapes into sandwiches at lunchtime.

Sunday dinner at our house is noticeably different than the other meals of the week. We always use a nice tablecloth and set folded napkins by each plate. It's a subtle reminder that Sunday is special. During dinner, we share missionary experiences we have had that week. Knowing there will be an accounting helps us all be a little more missionary-minded. And years ago, my husband began a Sunday dinner tradition of asking the children what they learned at church that day. Each child shares stories, impressions, and thoughts about their various lessons. Comments made in class make splendid dinner conversation.

One day, when four-year-old Abram could not remember his lesson, I tried to help by asking whether the teacher had shown any pictures or told any stories. Finally, his eyes lit up as he enthusiastically responded, "Yes, she showed us a picture of the Holy Ghost." (We still wonder where his teacher got that picture!)

One of our children's most-anticipated meals is Valentine's Day. We set the table with a red and white heart tablecloth, colored napkins, and candles. (When I'm feeling really ambitious, we even use china and crystal.) I prepare a special meal that is sometimes eaten in courses and always by candlelight. A nicely set table completely changes the mood and creates an atmosphere for practicing proper etiquette. The children even behave better.

For breakfast on April Fools' Day, we have waffles with ice cream and fruit or banana splits, and for dinner we eat breakfast food. Last year, I set the table with our red and white Valentine tablecloth, paper Christmas plates, green napkins, and a bunny in a basket as a centerpiece—I came up with the idea at the last minute and literally threw it together serendipitously. Fortunately, this is the day that anything goes!

Several years ago, I decided to have a Passover meal at Easter time, doing a lot of research to make it as authentic as possible. Then I purchased a lamb roast and several other important food items. Before eating, we discussed the significance of the first Passover and the symbolism of the food we would be eating. We enjoyed it so much that it has become an important part of our Easter celebration.

And a long-time family favorite is our Christmas Eve *Inn at Bethlehem* meal. Dressed in robes and using only the dim light of candles and the wood stove, we sit on a blanket in the kitchen, eating our version of a traditional Jewish meal (tortillas with chicken salad, olives, make-believe goat cheese and milk, dates, figs, almonds, and grape juice). When the meal is over, we read the Christmas story from Luke, and then one by one we light battery-operated candles and share our gratitude for the Savior, discussing how *His* light makes the world a brighter place for us all. A mellow mood settles over the room as we reflect on the Savior's birth by the flickering glow of firelight, and we're all a little reluctant for it to end.

Last year, as Christmas approached and my youngest daughter anticipated the upcoming festivities, the event she mentioned most was our Christmas Eve meal. She talked at length about the food that would be served, the setting, and her personal sentiments. This meal seemed to mean more to her than the presents. Another child has long maintained that it is better than Christmas Day. That is some meal.

Keep It Simple

Let me assure you, not every meal at our place is gourmet delight or some extravagant celebration. We have eaten plenty of leftovers and last-minute concoctions. Sometimes the simplest meals fill the greatest need. The examples I have given are sprinkled throughout an entire year, and even when we try to make them special, someone is bound to be mad, sad, crying, giggling, fighting . . . or spilling his milk. The most important factor in determining the success of your family's dining experience is the mood, not the menu. Be sure to serve your young warriors generous portions of love and laughter.

Feeding your family should be more than foraging for food or "sitting alone and shoveling it in."[13] A meal eaten in solitude satisfies an appetite, but in the company of loved ones it becomes a banquet. Whether it's a sumptuous feast or a simple supper, eating together can be a scrumptious event. Bite by bite, meal after meal, you can fortify your family and your fortress. Give your children a taste of your time that will touch their hearts, fill their souls, and bless their lives.

Notes

1. Steven Gilham, personal correspondence.

2. Miriam Weinstein, *The Surprising Power of Family Meals*: *How Eating Together Makes Us Smarter, Stronger, Healthier, and Happier* (Hanover, New Hampshire: Steerforth, 2005).

3. Nancy Gibbs, "The Magic of the Family Meal," *Time*, posted June 4, 2006, accessed January 3, 2015, http://content.time .com/time/magazine/article/0,9171,1200760,00.html.

4. Ibid.

5. Ibid.

6. Ezra Taft Benson, "To the Mothers in Zion" (a fireside for parents, February 22, 1987).

7. Thomas S. Monson, "What Have I Done for Someone Today?" *Ensign*, November 2009.

8. Ibid.

9. Nancy Gibbs, "The Magic of the Family Meal."

10. Ibid.

11. Ibid.

12. Bruce Feiler, from *The Secrets of Happy Families*, as quoted in *Reader's Digest*, September 2014, 42.

13. Nancy Gibbs, "The Magic of the Family Meal."

Prayer~Scripture Study~Meals

Family Home Evening

Family Home Evening

"Thy children shall be taught of the Lord;
and great shall be the peace of thy children."

—3 Nephi 22:13

he attempts at my house to instruct our sometimes less-than-cooperative children span the
spectrum—from funny to frustrating to infuriating. For
many years, we faced the ongoing battle of trying to keep the
baby quiet, the two year old content, and the older children
cooperative—and still retain the Spirit. And more than once,
children have disappeared impolitely in the middle of a lesson
for an ill-timed drink of water or bathroom break. We even had
one son wander to the kitchen, rummage around in the pantry,
grab a bite to eat, and walk leisurely back to the living room,
munching contentedly. This, by the way, was our should-
have-known-better, could-have-waited ten year old, *not* the
two year old. I nearly glared a hole through him!

I remember well Elder David A. Bednar's timeless talk on
lessons that "did not always produce high levels of edification"
and his own trials of attempting to teach his children "amid
outbursts such as 'He's touching me!' 'Make him stop looking

at me!' 'Mom, he's breathing my air!'"[1] It is comforting to know that even an Apostle has struggled in this area.

The message for us all is this: do not quit, even when it seems impossible. One of my less impressive lessons was one I spent a good deal of time preparing and did everything I could to invite and maintain the Spirit. As we initiated the normal come-to-home-evening routine, I kept reminding myself that I couldn't get cranky when the children delayed or when they whined and wiggled and fussed and fidgeted as we tried to get started. As usual, they managed to be unmanageable, and I struggled to keep calm.

In the middle of the opening song, our two year old threw a tantrum, and my husband, thinking he was doing his part to maintain order, held her firmly on his lap. However, this only aggravated the problem, and her writhing and wriggling worsened. (Unfortunately, I had failed to inform him of my need to have the Spirit and to do whatever it took to avoid contention of any kind.) By the time the opening prayer ended, our daughter's defiance and my husband's determination to constrain her had escalated to full-scale conflict, and my blood pressure had risen accordingly. At that moment, I knew the Spirit was gone and would not be returning any time soon, and I was definitely in no state of mind to teach the lesson I had prepared. I ran to my room in tears, while the family sat in stunned silence—bringing an abrupt and unexpected conclusion to what was most likely the shortest family home evening ever.

Family Night Can Be Successful

Thankfully, not all of our lessons have ended so disastrously. Halfway through his eighth birthday, my young son came to me quite upset. "Mom, it's hard being eight. If Abram does something to make me mad, I can't call him *stupid* or bad words like that." For the past several weeks, we had been giving him the missionary lessons in preparation for his baptism and had made it very clear that he would soon be accountable for his sins. Somehow, somewhere, sometime, *something* was sinking in.

One special family night, we invited both sets of grandparents for a lesson on the plan of salvation. Starting in the barn (heaven), we explained that an earth had been prepared where they could learn and grow and practice righteous living, and then we sent them on their way. The grandparents "died" quite suddenly and disappeared into the house while the rest of us wandered around the yard for a while.

Eventually, we came to the basement (outer darkness), where we explained the plight of the people who ended up there. It was dark and creepy, so we didn't linger long. Our home has four levels, which it made it convenient to move from level to level, symbolically moving from one glory to another. Each level increased in light, and we paused to talk about the conditions for inheriting that kingdom. Upon reaching the "celestial kingdom", we were warmly greeted by the "deceased" grandparents, who were dressed in white. We concluded with our testimonies and our hopes that we would one day live as a family eternally. It was an extraordinary lesson.

Another time, my husband wound hundreds of yards of

rope around the trees in our backyard. Blindfolded, we had to find our way from the beginning to the end with only the slight sound of a tinkling bell as a guide. When everyone finally made it, my husband gave a lesson on how listening to the Holy Ghost will lead us back to our heavenly home.

In contrast to my *less impressive* lesson, one of my more memorable lessons was a treasure hunt that taught the importance of choices. I started out by offering them a choice between a sealed envelope and some candy. They chose the candy. A note with candy led them down to the laundry room and their next clue. Again, they had a choice between the envelope and more candy. They chose the candy. The attached note led to the basement, where they again had a choice between the envelope and substantially more candy. They chose the candy. The final note led to a treasure box and the hopeful anticipation of finding a fortune. Excitedly, they opened it—only to find it filled with cow manure! They chose poorly.

After a few melancholy moments, we opened the envelope. It contained one dollar and a clue leading back upstairs to another envelope. That envelope contained ten dollars and another clue, leading up another flight of stairs. The third envelope was behind the family proclamation, bulging with one hundred dollars and the final clue. The grand prize—*one thousand dollars*—was hidden behind a picture of the Savior. You can imagine our children's genuine disappointment when they realized what they had given up in exchange for candy and cow manure. That night, they learned two extremely valuable lessons: choices have consequences and not everything that glitters is gold.

While some of our lessons have been successful, please don't imagine for a second that we've mastered the art of family home evening. With ten children—are you kidding?! We have had more than our share of skirmishes while trying to create unforgettable mentoring moments. Let me remind you that not all of our lessons have been (or are) as elaborate or successful.

These positive examples are few and far between. Most Monday nights are filled with simple gospel discussions in the living room, with an opening and closing song and prayer. That's it. Nothing fancy or earth-shattering. And, I hate to admit it, but sometimes we don't even have treats—a mild form of torture—but it has actually happened. Teaching and testifying are the most important aspects this evening, which can be done in small and simple ways, and children will learn.

What Works?

When the First Presidency initiated the family home evening program in 1915, parents were encouraged to set aside one night a week as family time. A century later, families still struggle to heed this advice. Why does it seem so hard? I have a few thoughts. First, children don't always want to be gathered for formal family time. Second, parents don't enjoy gathering children who refuse to be gathered. Third, in our trying-to-do-it-all world, this sometimes exasperating task is an easy one to eliminate. After all, in the short term, the consequences seem so inconsequential. And fourth, even for children who are willing to be gathered and parents who are intent on gathering, preparing a lesson that will keep the interest of everyone involved is challenging and time-consuming—unlike family prayer and scripture study, which require little advance preparation. And even with the most careful planning, we still end up with children who are mad, sad, crying, giggling, fighting . . . or eating. I am all too familiar with the difficulty of dealing with irritable teens and toddlers during what should be happy family time. But after these many years, I do have three suggestions for finding increased success.

One, begin early. I will be forever grateful to my oldest son's Sunbeam teacher who taught a lesson on family home evening when he was just three years old. He came home asking that we schedule this event the next day, creating a habit that has continued for more than a quarter of a century. Those first lessons were short and sweet, and I can still remember some of them. If your children are older, there is no better time to start than now. It is never too late and, as they say, better late than never.

Two, be consistent. Give your children something they can count on. If your children know that Monday night is family night, you have won half the battle. In fact, you will not dare miss because your little ones will remind you regularly. Family night was a highlight of our youngest daughter's week for many years (I hope it still is). With eagerness in her voice, she would come to me several times on Monday, reminding me that she was *so* excited for that evening. There was no way we could miss having it.

Three, make it fun. Give them something to look forward to, not something to dread. Give lessons, not lectures. A successful lesson does not end with children slouching dismally in their seats while listening to dull parents drone on indefinitely. Your children deserve better than that. Use attention-getters or short object lessons to generate interest—role play or tell stories, your own or others'. There are clever ways to give gospel messages that are enlightening and entertaining.

An *Ensign* article by the Sunday School general presidency offered some excellent suggestions for improving the quality of our lessons:

> Love those you teach. Seek after the one. Focus on the needs of your [children].
>
> Prepare yourself spiritually. Live what you teach. Know available resources.
>
> Teach by the Spirit. Help your [children] recognize the Spirit. Be a teachable teacher. Create a learning atmosphere.
>
> Discover the gospel together. Set high expectations. Encourage [children] to testify. Ask effective questions. Listen to your [children].
>
> Teach the doctrine. Use the scriptures. Use stories and examples. Promise blessings and testify.
>
> Invite [children] to act. Help your [children] practice. Follow up on invitations. [One family we know uses dinnertime to discuss how they are doing on their invitations to act.][2]

Even though we tried to make our lessons engaging, when the children were younger, we often got complaints about having a lesson again. Our children seemed to interpret *family night* to mean *fun night*. Finally, we implemented a monthly plan suggested by a friend: the first week Dad taught a lesson, the second week Mom, and the third week a child. The fourth week was an activity. The children knew exactly what to expect and when, and it cut down on the complaints considerably. It also helped my husband and I prepare better.

As more children became part of our ever-widening home evening circle, it became increasingly more difficult to keep everyone's attention. We found it worked best when we involved everyone in some way. Two year olds love to help—holding pictures, passing out paper and pencils, leading music, or saying prayers. Older children can prepare or help teach a lesson. When a child prepares a lesson, not only does his or her understanding of gospel principles increase, but he or she learns how important it is for others to listen and participate.

Activity nights are usually held at home with little or no expense—playing hide-and-seek or sardines in the dark (it's much more intense with the lights off); carving jack-o'-lanterns; hunting for Easter eggs; or playing basketball, baseball, or Ultimate Frisbee in the backyard. Other times we use these nights to work together in the yard or garden; bottle and preserve food; write letters to our missionaries and others; or serve members of our ward, neighborhood, or extended family.

Several years ago, we started a tradition of having conference quizzes the Monday following general conference. With a house full of intensely competitive personalities, this event is always eagerly anticipated. Knowing there will be a quiz with opposing teams has generated greater interest in conference and more careful listening. The children even take notes!

Occasionally, there are trips away from home for picnics, movies, swimming, or other activities. However, we have learned that there are good times to be had within our own family fortress. *Fun* and *free* can exist simultaneously.

And don't overlook the learning that can occur even on activity nights. After going to see the Christmas lights for a family home evening activity, a little girl asked her parents, "So what was it about?" Initially, they were not sure what she was really asking, so they told her they had just gone to have a good time. But their daughter persisted, "No, what was it about?" It was then that her parents realized that she was looking for a lesson in their experience.[3] They quickly came up with a short message on the meaning of Christmas to satisfy her desire to be taught, but it was the parents who learned the most valuable lesson of all: children yearn to learn. In the right setting and circumstance, any event can become a teaching moment.

And finally, it goes without being said that the best family home evenings end with something yummy. I once heard a mother, who was too busy to bake or buy any treats, tell of her son's sincere disappointment upon discovering the perceived tragedy. "Why did we even have home evening?" he retorted bitterly.

Despite the unwritten policy on Monday night treats, I must confess that they have not always been my top priority, especially when we had a house full of toddlers. Some days, preparing a treat was just the thing to put me over the top, and sometimes I included the treat as part of the evening meal— before the lesson—so we could use the same plates, cups, and forks, saving extra clean up later when I would be diapering and dressing children for bed.

And what do we do when our children get married or move away? It can become a little more difficult to foster unity under new family dynamics. Some families meet once a month for home evening or every Sunday for dinner. My family does not meet that frequently, but we do get together for birthdays, special family meals, backyard barbecues, and other events such as the county fair, circus, or rodeo. A few years ago, we started having get-togethers with our young adult and married children, discussing specific gospel topics without the interruption of the younger children. (Fortunately, our two youngest daughters love to babysit.) Sharing spiritual experiences is a powerful way to build unity with extended family members.

Never Give Up!

At the risk of being repetitive, let me reiterate that teaching your children need not be traumatic. Don't worry that you are not a gospel scholar. Your stewardship as a parent qualifies you for divine guidance. Remember, your children are God's children too. Knock boldly on heaven's door, seeking help for the challenges you face. You are entitled to wisdom beyond your own and inspiration that is relevant to your family relationships. "Every [parent] can be a gospel doctrine instructor in [his or] her home."[4]

There are several instances in the Book of Mormon where the preaching of the word made an impact. In fact, Alma stepped down as chief judge to be a full-time missionary and bring the people back to Christ. "And now, as the preaching of the word had a great tendency to lead the people to do that which was just—yea, it had had more powerful effect upon the minds of the people than the sword, or anything else, which had happened unto them—therefore Alma thought it was expedient that they should try the virtue of the word of God"

(Alma 31:5). He saw no way to "reclaim them save it were in bearing down in pure testimony against them" (Alma 4:19).

Alma knew what Boyd K. Packer knew: "True doctrine, understood, changes attitudes and behavior. The study of the doctrines of the gospel will improve behavior quicker than a study of behavior will improve behavior."[5]

A number of years ago, we were concerned about the activities of one of our children. My husband and I spoke with her privately, but it was obvious she did not agree with our counsel. I wondered how to help her understand. At length, I decided to teach a home evening lesson on that topic. I reasoned that by including all the children in the conversation, she would not feel picked on. I prayed and pondered, seeking help on how to approach it and what issues to include.

One day as I went about my daily chores, I had some strong impressions. In fact, a flood of thoughts came to me quite suddenly. *This is good stuff*, I thought excitedly. Specific phrases came into my mind, and I even thought of a story that summed up perfectly the point I was trying to make. Not wanting to forget anything, I quickly jotted my thoughts onto a piece of paper, arranging them later in logical order to form an outline from my notes. As I planned the lesson, I felt impressed to save one particular phrase for the end.

From that outline, we had a wonderful family discussion that included excellent comments from our children, validating many of the points my husband and I were trying to make. Everyone participated—except our daughter. She sat quietly in a defensive posture, staring at the floor most of the time. Later that evening, I lamented that I had not reached the one person I had hoped to reach and went to bed feeling like a failure.

During general conference a few weeks later, two of the talks were on the same topic as my lesson. In fact, one of them used some of the same phrases I had been inspired to use almost word for word. I listened in wonder as the speaker repeated my family home evening lesson to the entire Church! I was amazed at how the Spirit works and most grateful for this second witness. *Maybe she will listen when a General Authority says it*, I contemplated hopefully.

While preparing for bed a few days later, she came into my room to thank me for my lesson, admitting she had been wrong. *She's only apologizing because she heard it in conference*, I thought skeptically, so I asked, "Did you change your mind because of what you heard in conference?"

"Partly," she admitted. "But I had already changed my mind before that." She confessed that she was angry and unaffected during most of my lesson, but my closing comment—the one the Spirit had prompted me to save until the end—really touched her, and she had thought a lot about it.

Never give up! Teach truth even when it seems they aren't listening and even when they "resist the teaching and resent the teacher."[6] "Teach ye diligently and [Christ's] grace shall attend you" (D&C 88:78). Your children hear more than they let on, and you never know when something you say will soften a heart and save a soul. "There is a desperate need . . . to help our youth learn to understand, love, value, and live the standards of the gospel. Parents and youth must stand together in defense against a clever and devious adversary. We must be just as dedicated, effective, and determined in our efforts to live the gospel as he is in his efforts to destroy it—and us."[7]

Satan Does Not Want Us to Succeed

Children need to know that Satan has perfected the art of finding the chinks in their armor, and if they play in his court too long he will win. "There is a line of demarkation . . . between the Lord's territory and the devil's. . . . [If they] cross to the devil's side of the line one inch, [they] are in the tempter's power, and if he is successful, [they] will not be able to think or even reason properly."[8]

Satan is a liar. He loves to deceive, defraud, delude, and distort, and he will do anything to deaden our senses. He is an expert at disguise and camoflauge. Triumph over the devil's distortions includes helping our young soldiers strategically draw a line in the sand.

Dare to speak out. We must be the voice of reason amidst the shrill cries of a world clamoring for our children's attention. Never hesitate to raise that warning voice. God needs *us* to be *His* voice. Don't be afraid to testify of truth and relate personal experiences; sharing your own stories and bearing witness of them builds faith and invites the Spirit. Your children need to know that you know. They need to know what you know and how you know it. They may try to dispute doctrine, but they will find it difficult to dismiss the feelings of the Spirit. "May those we teach glimpse in us something of the Master Teacher and come away from the experience not merely informed, but transformed."[9]

"Remember the worth of souls is great in the sight of God; . . . and if it so be that you should labor all your days in crying repentance unto this people, and bring, save it be one soul unto me, how great shall be your joy with him in the kingdom of my Father!" (D&C 18:10, 15). The worth of a soul is the price you are willing to pay for it. What price are you willing to pay to save your own precious children?

Called to Teach

President Ezra Taft Benson declared, "You are your children's best teacher. . . . A [parent's] love and prayerful concern for [their] children are [their] most important ingredients in teaching [their] own. . . . [Parents], teach your children the gospel in your own home, at your own fireside. This is the most effective teaching that your children will ever receive. This is the Lord's way of teaching . . . and the Lord will sustain you."[10]

Teaching children is not reserved for formal moments only. We can teach while preparing food, driving in a vehicle, folding laundry, and sitting quietly alone with a child. Don't relinquish this most important role to others.

Former Relief Society General President Julie B. Beck told of a friend who commented that "he did not learn anything at church that he had not already learned at home. His parents used family scripture study, prayer, family home evening, mealtimes, and other gatherings to teach." She concluded, "Think of the power of our future missionary force if [parents] considered their homes as a pre-missionary training center. Then the doctrines of the gospel taught in the MTC would be a review and not a revelation."[11] During quiet reflective moments, we might ask ourselves, "How much of the gospel would [my] children know, if all they knew is what they had been taught at home?"[12] That is a sobering question to ponder.

Speaking on the power of teaching, President Henry B. Eyring said,

> A wise parent would never miss a chance to gather children together to learn of the doctrine of Jesus Christ. Such moments are so rare in comparison with the efforts of the enemy. For every hour the power of doctrine is introduced into a child's life, there may be hundreds of hours of messages and images denying or ignoring the saving truths.
>
> The question should not be whether we are too tired to prepare to teach doctrine or whether it wouldn't be better to draw a child closer by just having fun or whether the child isn't beginning to think that we preach too much. The question must be, "With so little time and so few opportunities, what words of doctrine from me will fortify them against the attacks on their faith which are sure to come?" The words you speak today may be the ones they remember. And today will soon be gone.[13]

Today will soon be gone. Those words have haunted me since I first heard them spoken years ago. If not me, who? If not now, when? Some days when I am really busy and tempted to do something fun rather than prepare a lesson, I remember this counsel, and it inspires me to do more. "The world will teach our children if we do not, and children are capable of learning all the world will teach them at a very young age. What we want them to know five years from now needs to be part of our conversation with them today."[14]

85

Teach Doctrine

Counseling parents, Elder Richard G. Scott admonished, "Be cautious not to make your family home evening just an afterthought of a busy day. . . . Don't let employment demands, sports, extracurricular activities, homework, or anything else become more important than that time you spend together at home with your family."[15]

This brings us to the million-dollar question: With all the prophetic promises and counsel regarding family home evening, why do we still allow community activities to dominate Monday night? Even when we participate as a family, is the family *all* together, and are we teaching doctrine? In the difficult days we live in—with the big bad wolf literally coming through our walls and boldly prowling about inside our homes—it is no longer enough just to be together. That will not save our children. We must "talk of Christ, . . . rejoice in Christ, . . . [and] preach of Christ" (2 Nephi 25:26). Our children must know how to "come unto Christ, and be perfected in Him" (Moroni 10:32). We simply cannot do that on a soccer field, a dance floor, a basketball court, or in a rodeo arena.

Family home evening is a program with a promise. When it was introduced years ago, the First Presidency declared, "If the Saints obey this counsel, we promise that great blessings will result. Love at home and obedience to parents will increase. Faith will be developed in the hearts of the youth of Israel, and they will gain power to combat the evil influences and temptations which beset them."[16]

Combating evil—that's what it's all about. Our greatest responsibility as parents is to produce warriors who have the physical, mental, spiritual, and emotional capacity to wage war on wickedness. Don't underestimate the dark side; Satan is no amateur. He has had centuries to master his craft, and victory over his special forces will require our most diligent efforts. He knows how important family night is and the incredible power that comes into a home when parents and children study the gospel together. He will do anything to disrupt, distract, destroy, or discourage your attempts to teach your children. Consistently having family home evening may not be a small or simple undertaking, but lesson after lesson, we build spiritual armor for our children and provide increased confidence for their encounters with evil. It is a critical defense strategy for deflecting the devil's malicious agenda.

Notes

1. David A. Bednar, "More Diligent and Concerned at Home," *Ensign*, November 2009.

2. Tad R. Callister, John S. Tanner, and Devin G. Durrant, "What Manner of Teachers Ought We to Be?" *Ensign*, January 2015, 63.

3. Steven Gilham, personal correspondence.

4. Julie B. Beck, "Seek Education and Lifelong Learning," *Ensign*, August 2009, 61.

5. Boyd K. Packer, "Little Children," *Ensign*, November 1986.

6. Boyd K. Packer, "Teaching Gospel Principles to Children," *Marriage and Family Relations, Participant's Study Guide* (Salt Lake City: Intellectual Reserve, 2000), 61.

7. M. Russell Ballard, "Guiding Children as They Make Decisions," *Marriage and Family Relations, Participant's Study Guide*, 64.

8. George Albert Smith, as quoted in Spencer W. Kimball, *The Miracle of Forgiveness* (Salt Lake City: Bookcraft, 1977), 232.

9. Tad R. Callister, John S. Tanner, and Devin G. Durrant, "What Manner of Teachers Ought We to Be?"

10. Ezra Taft Benson, "To the Mothers in Zion" (a fireside for parents, February 22, 1987).

11. Julie B. Beck, "Mothers Who Know," *Ensign*, November 2007.

12. A. Theodore Tuttle, as quoted in Gene R. Cook, *Raising Up a Family to the Lord* (Salt Lake City: Deseret Book, 1993), 25.

13. Henry B. Eyring, "The Power of Teaching Doctrine," *Ensign*, May 1999.

14. Rosemary M. Wixom, "Lighting Our Children's Path with Gospel Standards," *Ensign,* August 2015, 44; emphasis added.

15. Richard G. Scott, "Make the Exercise of Faith Your First Priority," *Ensign,* November 2014, 94.

16. The First Presidency, "Family Home Evening: Counsel and a Promise," *Ensign*, June 2003.

Prayer~~Scripture Study~~Meals~~Home Evening

Family Traditions

Family Traditions

"Therefore . . . stand fast, and hold the
traditions which ye have been taught."

—2 Thessalonians 2:15

One of my family's most unusual traditions is our
Fourth of July habit of having some major outdoor
project to complete as temperatures are topping out at one
hundred degrees—or more! The first time this happened was
several years ago, when my husband determined that the
roof needed replacing. He got a special deal on shingles and
decided that the best time to begin would be over the holiday when all the children would be home to help. There we
were, perched miserably atop the house while sirens blared
in the distance, signaling the start of our town's patriotic
parade.

The project took longer than expected, and before it was
complete, my husband and a couple of our sons had to leave
for a weeklong Scout camp. Those who remained at home
continued roofing with the rather ambitious aim of finishing
before they returned. We barely made it. The last shingles were
put into place as they pulled into the driveway.

A few years later, we reroofed our very tall, oversized barn during the same holiday, and two years ago, we equipped our half-acre lawn with a long overdue sprinkling system. Last year, we once again celebrated this occasion by working on an outdoor project with our extended family. (That is one tradition we should definitely discontinue!)

Nevertheless, by working together, we have grown closer. Work is an important part of our family's culture. We have remodeled several rooms in the house, including the kitchen, and have taught the children how to maintain a home and yard. Every summer, we grow a large garden and spend several months canning, drying, juicing, and jamming produce. We also have a small farm that requires the continuing care of livestock, clearing ditches, hauling hay, and repairing fences. But it has also created many happy memories, huddling around newborn animals in the barn.

Another tradition is all the children sleeping in the basement on Christmas Eve. This began years ago with the purchase of our first home. Up to this point, all the children had shared the same room in tiny, two-bedroom apartments. Even though our new home had an additional bedroom, they insisted on bunking in together for Christmas Eve. That first year, there were five of them, then six . . . seven . . . and eventually eight children, all crowded into one small room. At this rate, we wondered how long this tradition could survive! Gratefully, the home we currently own has a family room in the basement that is large enough for all ten children, a couple of spouses, and the grandchildren.

Going on family walks is another ritual that started with

that first stroller ride decades ago. When we lived in Hawaii, our home was just down the street from the Laie Hawaii Temple, and we walked to and from that sacred spot many times. The little community in which we now live has blocks a half mile long—two miles around each block—so we have traded our walking shoes for wheels and have spent many pleasant summer evenings pedaling bikes around town.

We have also taken the children on several long vacations, including trips to Disneyland and some Church historical sites. But one of our favorite getaways is a camping spot just up the canyon, near a reservoir that provides all the essentials of a great time together: campfires, canoeing, and cliff jumping.

And one of my favorite mothering traditions is reading to my children, from toddler to teenager. We have read lots of books, over and over. For years, it was part of our daily routine. As the children grew older, we read novels as a family, with Mom or Dad reading aloud. Through books, we have traveled far and wide and gone on marvelous adventures without ever leaving home. Reading stimulates the brain's ability to function and focus more than many of the conventional activities available to children. It is also a great way to keep them entertained and quiet while traveling.

Other family traditions include Christmas caroling to neighbors, Sabbath day activities (reading Church magazines, journal writing, scripture study, Personal Progress, Duty to God, writing to missionaries, indexing, family councils, scrapbooking, and so on), visits to widows in our ward, special family meals, service projects, homemade ice cream, and the county fair. And, thanks to our son-in-law, we are now getting to know our children's spouses while playing some pretty intense games around the kitchen table. But, regardless of what we do, we can usually count on someone being mad, sad, crying, giggling, fighting . . . or overheating on some Fourth of July project.

What Are Traditions?

Traditions are customs, habits, practices, activities, routines, or rituals performed on a regular basis. They can be large or small, simple or complex. They can be done inside or outside the home (or at other locations). But we must carefully consider the traditions we choose to create within our families because they have lasting consequences.

Remember, it was the wicked traditions of Laman and Lemuel that led their children and grandchildren and future generations into apostasy. And it was the traditions of parents during New Testament times that led their posterity astray. "And it came to pass that the children . . . gave heed to the traditions of their fathers and believed not the gospel of Christ, wherein they became unholy" (D&C 74:4). Our children are entitled to a heritage free from the false traditions of their fathers.

Righteous traditions, on the other hand, keep our families close to each other and the Lord. Elder L. Tom Perry suggested some "holy habits"[1] we should adopt: daily prayer and scripture study, weekly family home evening and Sabbath day observance, monthly fasts and payment of tithes and offerings, semiannual listening to general conference, and annual family reunions. "Other traditions . . . are receiving father's blessings, patriarchal blessings, missionary preparation, temple preparation, and regular temple attendance where possible, and being together as family units on those occasions when sacred ordinances are performed. . . . If we will build righteous traditions in our families, the light of the gospel can grow ever brighter in the lives of our children from generation to generation."[2]

Sabbath Tradition

Increasingly, honoring the Sabbath day is being recognized as a vital part of our worship. I think of the Sabbath as a tithing of our time. Just as we give the Lord one tenth of our income, we should give Him one day each week. President Harold B. Lee likened the failure to honor this day as "losing a soul full of joy in return for a thimble full of pleasure."[3]

Since the Creation, there has been a Sabbath. God was the first to honor it. "For in six days the Lord made heaven and earth, and on the seventh day he rested, and was refreshed" (Exodus 31:17). The number seven is symbolic of wholeness, completion, and perfection. Therefore, God rested on the seventh day, when the world was complete. Likewise, our resting one day in seven "creates a new and holy man [or woman]"[4] and is an essential aspect of our eventual perfection. "The concept of sanctification and the idea of rest as used in the scriptures seem closely related. . . . God's *work* is the sanctification of his children to the point where they can enter into the ultimate *rest*, which is the fulness of [God's] glory."[5]

The Sabbath is a "perpetual covenant" (Exodus 31:16) between God and His people "throughout [their] generations" (Exodus 31:13). This two-way promise includes remarkable blessings, as outlined by Isaiah:

If thou turn away thy foot from the Sabbath, from doing thy pleasure on my holy day; and call the Sabbath a delight, the holy of the Lord, honourable; and shalt honour him, not doing thine own ways, nor finding thine own pleasure, nor speaking thine own words:

Then shalt thou delight thyself in the Lord; and I will cause thee to ride upon the high places of the earth, and feed thee with the heritage of Jacob thy father: for the mouth of the Lord hath spoken it. (Isaiah 58:13–14; emphasis added)

Note the *if-then* structure of those verses. The first verse is our part of the covenant and is pretty straightforward; the second verse, however, requires some searching to fully understand. I have discovered that "delight[ing] thyself in the Lord" is similar to having "thy confidence wax strong in the presence of God (D&C 121:45)"[6]; that "rid[ing] upon the high places" means prosperity (see Deuteronomy 32:13–14; Habakkuk 3:19), protection (see Deuteronomy 33:29), and spiritual peace and power[7]; and that the "heritage of Jacob" is exaltation (see Doctrine and Covenants 132:37). Therefore, *if* we *honor, delight, and do God's will* on this day, *then* He will bless us with *peace, prosperity, protection, and exaltation.* As always, God gives far more than He expects in return.

This covenant was renewed in the latter days through revelation given to Joseph Smith:

And that thou mayest more fully keep thyself unspotted from the world, thou shalt go to the house of prayer and offer up thy sacraments upon my holy day;

For verily this is a day appointed unto you to rest from your labors, and to pay thy devotions unto the Most High; . . .

But remember that on this, the Lord's day, thou shalt offer thine oblations and thy sacraments. . . .

And on this day thou shalt do none other thing, only let thy food be prepared with singleness of heart that thy fasting may be perfect, or, in other words, that thy joy may be full.

Verily, this is fasting and prayer, or in other words, rejoicing and prayer.

And inasmuch as ye do these things with thanksgiving, with cheerful hearts and countenances, not with much laughter, for this is sin, but with a glad heart and a cheerful countenance. . . .

The fulness of the earth is yours . . . even peace in this world, and eternal life in the world to come. (D&C 59:9–10, 12–16, 23)

Do you see the *if-then* structure? *If* we go to church, partake of the sacrament, rest from our labors, offer our oblations, prepare our food with singleness of heart, and have a cheerful countenance—*honor, delight, and do God's will*—*then* we will keep ourselves unspotted from the world, have the fulness of the earth, and have peace in this world and eternal life in the world to come—*peace, prosperity, protection, and exaltation.*

After studying the law of the Sabbath at some length, I have come to several conclusions. First, using the term *Sabbath* rather than *Sunday* helps to set it apart in significant ways from the other days of the week.

Second, our three-hour Sabbath schedule is an inspired plan from God's prophet, and "go[ing] to the house of prayer" means attending all three meetings.

Third, "[preparing food] with singleness of heart" was not placed there accidentally. I have thought much about what this means and why God would include it as part of the covenant. Making a meal can be a lot of work. God wants His day to be a *spiritual* feast. He plainly taught this principle as the Israelites journeyed in the wilderness. Every day, they collected manna. If they gathered more than necessary for one day, the excess spoiled. However, the day before the Sabbath, they collected enough for two days without any spoilage. Pondering this principle has caused a change in my family's Sabbath day meal preparations—planning food that can mostly be made ahead of time. In addition to baking and cooking, there is much that can be done the day before to minimize our labors on this holy day. As the children's song says, "Saturday is a special day. It's the day we get ready for Sunday."[8]

Fourth, "my conduct and my attitude on the Sabbath [constitute] a *sign* between me and my Heavenly Father."[9] How well we hallow this day is a reflection of our love for God. In addition to being a day of rest, renewal, and refreshment from our daily tasks, it is a day to remember Him. Perhaps that is why Satan tries so hard to make us forget. Offering our oblations entails giving our time, talents, and means to God and others (see D&C 59:12). Is it really too difficult to cheerfully spend one day each week in His service?

Most of us do pretty well when it comes to the public keeping of this holy day—attending church and abstaining from shopping, working in our yards, and other recreational activities. But what about our private observance—those things we do *inside* our homes? That's where it really counts. It's not about impressing others; it's about honoring God. Do we spend our private time lounging about or leisurely puttering around with lesser things, or are we "anxiously engaged" in *His* work (D&C 58:27)? He is always watching.

And fifth, God really wants our undivided attention on the Sabbath. It is, after all, His day. Amidst the thunder of Mount Sinai, the Lord wrote ten commandments upon tablets of stone. Several of these occupy only a single sentence, but, interestingly,ß the command to honor the Sabbath covers four verses. Furthermore, the penalty under the law of Moses for disregarding this day was death (see Exodus 31:14–15; Numbers 15:32–36).

Fortunately for us all, stoning people to death is no longer the punishment for violating this holy day, but failure to honor it does lead to our *spiritual* demise. If fully observing the Sabbath has been an overlooked part of your family worship, you should consider including it. It is in the home that children learn the deepest meanings of keeping this covenant. It is a ritual that will bless your family now and into the eternities.

Creating Righteous Traditions

Our children are entitled to a heritage rich in gospel traditions. Of necessity, this means being selective in how we spend our time. When the children of Israel left Egypt, they struggled to stay focused on the basics of gospel living, so the Lord established strict rules and rituals to be observed on a daily basis to help them remember Him. *Latter-day* saints are not required to follow the same customs as the people who lived under the Law of Moses, but our family traditions do help determine how well we remember God.

Perhaps we should pause long enough to consider whether we are "building a strong foundation of righteous traditions that our children can depend on."[10] In a conference talk enti-tled "Righteous Traditions," Cheryl Lant, former Primary general president, encouraged us to ask some serious questions: "What kinds of traditions do we have? Are they what we want them to be? . . . Are they based on actions of righteousness and faith? Are they mostly material in nature, or are they eternal? Are we consciously creating righteous traditions, or is life just happening to us? Are our traditions being created in response to the loud voices of the world, or are they influenced by the still, small voice of the Spirit? . . . Will [our children's] hearts and lives be full of traditions that make it easy for them to accept and follow the Lord and the latter-day prophets?"[11] These candid questions deserve careful consideration.

"Just because something is *good* is not a sufficient reason for doing it," explains Elder Dallin H. Oaks. "Parents should act to preserve time for family prayer, family scripture study, family home evening, and the other precious togetherness . . . that binds a family together and fixes children's values on things of eternal worth."[12]

Linda S. Reeves, second counselor in the Relief Society gen-eral presidency, was told by a friend that it stresses women out when they are asked to read the scriptures and pray because they already have too much to do. In response, Sister Reeves shared her experience of raising her own children. She found increased peace as she changed her focus from "the less-important things" to a gospel-centered home. "I must testify of the blessings of daily scripture study and prayer and weekly family home even-ing. These are the very practices that help take away stress, give direction to our lives, and add protection to our homes."[13]

Other Traditions

In addition to our righteous traditions, there are a host of other habits that cultivate harmony among family members. These activities "create meaningful family bonds that give [our] children an identity stronger than what they can find with their peer group or at school or anyplace else."[14] Some of these include birthdays, holidays, mealtimes, vacations, camping, and recreational activities. These shared memories contribute to a family's culture, foster unity, and forge friendships.

But we must choose wisely. Elder M. Russell Ballard told the story of a mother whose children were involved in twenty-nine various activities every week. Exhausted and exasperated, she finally called a family meeting and declared, "Something has to go; we have no time to ourselves and no time for each other." Extracurricular activities can quickly overwhelm our families, therefore, it is crucial that we consciously create time for one another. As Elder Ballard counseled, "Families need unstructured time in which relationships can deepen and real parenting can take place."[15]

When you are together, make sure everyone is *really* there. Don't allow meaningless electronic amusements to consume special family time. We can become slaves to our equipment by being continually at the beck and call of the trite and trivial, or by residing in some virtual reality. What good does it do to marshal the forces, and then have everyone electronically disengaged from the event? One mother became so frustrated with this problem when her extended family gathered that she now has everyone deposit their cell phones in a basket by the front door when they arrive. Another mother told of her extreme disappointment when her father missed hearing his only grandchild say "grandpa" for the first time because he was distracted with his phone. There is nothing quite so deflating as having a device become more important than the ones we are with. We could all benefit from a few lessons on electronic etiquette.

Wise parents "are selective about their own activities and involvement to conserve their limited strength in order to maximize their influence where it matters most. . . . They permit less of what will not bear good fruit eternally. They allow less media in their homes, less distraction, less activity that draws their children away from their home. . . . [They] choose carefully and do not try to choose it all."[16] If our family traditions do not allow us to fulfill our most important responsibilities, we may need to rethink our priorities. In other words, if we are too busy for what matters most, we are too busy!

Do Not Become Distracted

Satan is the master distracter. He knows that the chances of getting you or me to commit a serious sin are so slim that he doesn't even tempt us with those things. He is much too clever to waste his time on pathetic, ineffective persuasions, opting instead for more elusive enticements. Slowly and subtly, he skillfully seduces us to fill our lives with so many *good* things that there is no longer room for the *best* things. It is a cunning ploy, and we must be extremely careful about becoming caught in this deceptive snare.

Childhood is a once-in-a-lifetime experience, and there should definitely be time for some of the nonessentials. However, our responsibility as parents is to prepare our children for the time that follows childhood since that is where the majority of their lives will be spent. Some of these extracurricular activities are nice *if* we can afford them—financially, spiritually, and emotionally. However, if they are draining our bank accounts or taking a toll on our mental, physical, or familial wellbeing, they are not worth the cost. "Things which matter most must never be at the mercy of things which matter least."[17]

Years ago, my husband and I deliberated at length on this. We set long-term goals for our family and how we wanted to spend our time and money and planned accordingly. Before entering into new endeavors, we carefully consider whether it will bring us closer to each other, our children, and the Lord.

Part of this plan included selling my husband's beloved bagpipes to purchase a piano for the family. Selflessly, he replaced his prized possession for something we considered a higher priority. While listening to one of the children playing a particularly beautiful piano piece recently, he realized that his sacrifice had not been in vain.

In addition to playing the piano, our children have, on a limited basis, been involved in dance, wrestling, basketball, and track. Of our ten children, we've had one son play soccer one summer, when we lived close enough that he could walk to practice and the games. I realize that limiting *outside* involvement is a personal choice, but it has made all the difference *inside* our home.

Instead of spending Saturdays running from game to game, our family spends them working in the yard and garden, canning, cleaning house, sewing, and preparing food for the

Sabbath. And there is still time for jumping on the trampoline; riding bikes; or playing catch, soccer, or basketball in the backyard. Many summer evenings are spent hand cranking homemade ice cream and enjoying pleasant family time on the patio. We are all there together—leisurely chatting and enjoying each other's company. Sometimes it even turns into family Frisbee or a spontaneous game of kickball. The best part is that I don't have to buy any uniforms, pay any fees, or drive anywhere!

One of my happiest childhood memories was playing night games with the neighbors in my own backyard—tag, kick the can, or ghost tag (our all-time favorite). It brought us together as children and created memories that I cherish to this day. In our technology-absorbed world, I wonder whether our children are losing the ability and the desire to play, or whether they are so overscheduled that they just don't have the time. A return to the activities of yesteryear will not only produce more picturesque Norman Rockwell moments but will bring a greater measure of peace into our families' lives.

When Ron J. Turker, a pediatric orthopedic surgeon, told a teenage boy that he had torn his ACL in a sports injury and would need a minimum of six months to heal from a complicated medical procedure, the boy's mother exclaimed, "You don't understand, this is his life!" And his father demanded, "We need this fixed—he's in the Olympic Development Program! He's elite." Dr. Turker then went on to describe the dilemma created by this "new and lucrative paradigm" that parents have bought into.

Our kids no longer play sports; they are youth "athletes." The landscape of youth sports has changed markedly in the last 20 years. Free play, where children gather after school, pick a game and play until called in for dinner, is almost extinct. Highly organized and stratified sports have become the norm. Time, place and rules are now dictated to our kids rather than organized by the kids. . . . As parents, we want what's best for our kids but we've abdicated our parental rights and duties to the new societal norm. . . . We give in to the herd mentality . . . so that our kids won't be seen as outliers.[18]

Any virtue taken to an extreme can become a vice—dance or music lessons, classes, clubs, sports, hunting, hobbies, work, television, the Internet, and even time spent playing as a family or fulfilling Church callings. There must be balance and there must be purpose. Otherwise, we will be "tossed to and fro" (Ephesians 4:14) with every event that comes our way. Certainly, there are good things to be gained from nearly every endeavor, but each activity comes at the expense of something else. Would it not be wise, therefore, to carefully perform a cost-benefit analysis before proceeding?

Furthermore, the importance we place on some of these activities will fade with time. Children grow up and move on, and "today will soon be gone."[19] When today is gone, what is it you want *most* for your children? An honest evaluation will most likely begin and end with spiritual things, so why spend so much time on those things that aren't spiritual? What we really want in the long term must be the focus of the short term.

A Well-Balanced Spiritual Diet

Life is short; eat dessert first is an excellent example of short-term choosing. Said in jest, this popular phrase is intended to assuage our guilt over poor eating habits. However, the negative consequences to such behavior are obvious. A well-balanced diet is essential for building strong bones and bodies, and we all recognize the benefits of filling up on nutrient-rich food before consuming empty calories. Consequently, discriminating parents don't allow their children to head straight to the dessert bar of their local buffet or to gobble an endless supply of goodies. They wouldn't jeopardize their children's health so carelessly.

However, when it comes to feeding their spirits, we are sometimes not as vigilant. In today's topsy-turvy world, too many children are feasting at the dessert bar of life. Children need a regular diet of religious rations—generous helpings served daily. Nevertheless, it is easy to become complacent about their moral wellbeing because the negative effects of spiritual malnourishment often go undetected until our young warriors are too weak to fight off the ravenous wolves growling at our gates.

In an address given to seminary and institute leaders, President J. Reuben Clark Jr. emphasized this point: "The youth of the Church are hungry for things of the Spirit; they are eager to learn the gospel, and they want it straight, undiluted. . . . They want to gain testimonies. . . . [They] crave the faith their fathers and mothers have; they want it in its simplicity and purity. . . . [They] . . . are spiritually working . . . toward a maturity which they will early reach if you but feed them the right food."[20]

Before dishing up another helping of life's dessert for your children, ask yourself a few questions:

- Do I "spend excess time on ineffective activities that yield little spiritual sustenance"?[21]
- Do I place as much priority on the sacred as the secular?
- Am I vicariously living my life through my children's activities?
- Can I really afford the extra expense these events create?
- Do my children participate in some activities simply because all the children in the neighborhood, the ward, or the school do?
- Are my children participating in so many activities that they are not learning essential life skills: cooking, cleaning, budgeting, and serving others?
- Do they participate because I think it makes *me* a good parent?

Ironically, participation in too many extra activities does not make us good parents. We end up running here and there in a frazzled, frenzied state, stretched too thin to have sufficient time and energy for that which matters most. You simply cannot be all things to all people all the time without feeling like you've lost yourself.

Satan is extremely adept at sneaking behind enemy lines and sabotaging from within. He does not want your family to succeed. He knows that if he can create conflict and confusion or distractions and diversions, his chances of winning are greatly increased. Don't give up what you want most for what you think you want at the moment.

Building Family-Friendly Traditions

Some traditions can lead us away from the protecting walls of our family fortress or become so distracting as to hinder us from even building a fortress in the first place. Remember the third little pig. It was the meticulous, ongoing care he gave to his work that saved his life and the lives of his brothers. Likewise, our diligence in fortifying our family fortress may literally save our children from the *wicked wolf* and provide peace in a "war-weary, sin-laden world."[22]

Life's fondest memories or most worthwhile activities are not usually expensive or elaborate. Speaking of his childhood home, President Harold B. Lee said, "We had everything money could not buy."[23] And Elder Dallin H. Oaks told the story of a family who spent one summer going on several family trips. At the end of the summer when the father asked his teenage son which activity he liked most, the son replied, "The thing I liked best this summer . . . was the night you and I laid on the lawn and looked at the stars and talked."[24]

"Not everything that can be counted counts, and not every-thing that counts can be counted."[25] Providing quality experiences for your children does not necessarily require large quantities of cash or prolonged investments of time. Huge dividends can be gained from just being together for the simple, ordinary, daily tasks of life.

Whatever we choose to do as families, we must remember that not all traditions are of equal worth. Some are just for fun, and that is all right as long as they aren't encroaching on more important matters or causing us to overlook what matters most.

I suspect that in our final interview with the Savior, there are many activities He will not even question us about. However, I feel quite certain that our family teachings and traditions will be near the top of His evaluation.

Life-sustaining spiritual sustenance comes in the form of regular religious rituals. Teaching values and the things of eternity is the entrée of life; entertainment is the dessert. We must be careful that we don't get it backward. A little dessert tastes good, but too much of it will make us ill. You are what you eat!

Keeping Christ in Our Traditions

President Howard W. Hunter taught, "If our lives and our faith are centered on Jesus Christ and his restored gospel, nothing can ever go permanently wrong. On the other hand, if our lives are not centered on the Savior and his teachings, no other success can ever be permanently right."[26] And President Thomas S. Monson affirmed, "Before we can successfully undertake a personal search for Jesus, we must first prepare time for him in our lives and room for him in our hearts. In these busy days there are many who have time for golf, time for shopping, time for work, time for play—but no time for Christ."[27]

"Sometimes it feels like we are drowning in frivolous foolishness," warns Elder Quentin L. Cook. "Many choices are not inherently evil, but if they absorb all of our time and keep us from the best choices, then they become insidious. . . . We need to recognize that there is a seriousness of purpose that must undergird our approach to life and all our choices. Distractions and rationalizations that limit progress are harmful enough, but when they diminish faith in Jesus Christ . . . they are tragic."[28]

"To the Prophet Joseph Smith the Lord said, 'Your family must needs repent and forsake some things' (D&C 93:48). Each of our families is confronted with a broad menu of activities and entertainment, not all of which is wholesome and good—and much of which is certainly not necessary. . . . Do our families also need to repent and forsake some things to help us maintain the sacred nature of our homes? The establishment of our homes as holy places reflects the depth of sacrifice we are willing to make for them."[29] As we learn from the Lord's stern rebuke to Joseph Smith, God sees into our homes and knows what kind of children we are raising.

Educating children and establishing righteous traditions isn't just good parenting; it is a sacred trust. Indeed, it is a commandment: "Inasmuch as parents have children in Zion, or in any of her stakes . . . that teach them not to understand the doctrine of repentance, faith in Christ the Son of the living God, and of baptism and the gift of the Holy Ghost . . . when eight years old, the sin be upon the heads of the parents" (D&C 68:25). I don't need any of my children's sins—I have plenty of my own!

But despite our best efforts, some children still stray. There are no guarantees, even in the gospel. Our heavenly parents lost a multitude of children before any of us ever came to earth. This war that is being waged began in the realms above over agency—our ability to choose compliance or defiance. It is a sacred gift God will never take from us. Satan's plan was force, but the Savior stands with arms extended, ever beckoning and lovingly waiting for us to come to Him. As mortal parents, we must allow the children entrusted to our care the same privilege, as painful as it may be.

Brick by brick, however, we can do our part to bring them to Christ by creating wholesome and worthwhile traditions. These are the essential building blocks of a formidable fortress. The lifelong behaviors your family develops will, in large measure, determine the destiny of your children. Don't rob them of priceless opportunities to bolster faith and build testimony. In the end, it is our "holy habits"[30] that get us into heaven.

Notes

1. Becky Edwards, "Are you putting on the full armor of God every day? Holy habits are the key," *Purpose Driven Motherhood*, posted January 7, 2015, http://purposedrivenmotherhood .blogspot.com/2015/01/are-you-putting-on-full-armor-of-god .html.

2. L. Tom Perry, "Family Traditions," *Ensign*, May 1990.

3. Harold B. Lee, "The Calling of the Twelve," *The Life and Teachings of Jesus & His Apostles* (Salt Lake City: The Church of Jesus Christ of Latter-day Saints, 1979), 52.

4. *Old Testament Student Manual Genesis–2 Samuel* (Salt Lake City: Corporation of the President of The Church of Jesus Christ of Latter-day Saints, 1981), 130.

5. Ibid.; see also D&C 84:24.

6. *Old Testament Student Manual 1 Kings–Malachi,* (Salt Lake City: Corporation of the President of The Church of Jesus Christ of Latter-day Saints, 1981), 205.

7. Mountaintops were often places of revelation and inspiration—for examples, see Moses 1:1; 7:1; 1 Nephi 11:1; Ether 3:1; Isaiah 2:2.

8. Rita S. Robinson, "Saturday," *Children's Songbook* (Salt Lake City: Deseret Book, 1991), 196.

9. Russell M. Nelson, "The Sabbath Is a Delight," *Ensign*, May 2015.

10. Cheryl C. Lant, "Righteous Traditions," *Ensign*, May 2008.

11. Ibid.

12. Dallin H. Oaks, "Good, Better, Best," *Ensign*, November 2007.

13. Linda S. Reeves, "Protection from Pornography—a Christ-Focused Home," *Ensign*, May 2014.

14. M. Russell Ballard, "What Matters Most Is What Lasts Longest," *Ensign*, November 2005.

15. M. Russell Ballard, *Daughters of God* (Salt Lake City: Deseret Book, 2009), 10.

16. Julie B. Beck, "Mothers Who Know," *Ensign*, November 2007.

17. Johann Wolfgang von Goethe, *Goodreads*, accessed February 26, 2015, http://www.goodreads.com/quotes/2326-things-which-matter-most-must-never-be-at-the-mercy.

18. Ron J. Turker, "All Played Out," *The New York Times*, July 28, 2014, http://www.nytimes.com/2014/07/28/opinion/all-played-out.html.

19. Henry B. Eyring, "The Power of Teaching Doctrine," *Ensign*, May 1999.

20. J. Reuben Clark Jr., "The Charted Course of the Church in Education," address given to seminary and institute leaders,

Brigham Young University, August 8, 1938, https://www.lds
.org/bc/content/shared/content/english/pdf/language-materials
/32709_eng.pdf?lang=eng.

21. Dallin H. Oaks, "Good, Better, Best."

22. Howard W. Hunter, *Teachings of Presidents of the Church* (Salt
Lake City: Intellectual Reserve, 2015), 51.

23. Harold B. Lee, *Teachings of Presidents of the Church* (Salt Lake
City: Intellectual Reserve, 2000), xii.

24. Dallin H. Oaks, "Good, Better, Best."

25. Albert Einstein (attributed), *The Quotations Page*, accessed
March 2, 2015, http://www.quotationspage.com/quote/26950
.html.

26. Howard W. Hunter, as quoted by Laura F. Willes, *Christmas
with the Prophets* (Salt Lake City: Deseret Book, 2010), 10.

27. Thomas S. Monson, as quoted by Laura F. Willes, *Christmas
with the Prophets*, 12.

28. Quentin L. Cook, "Choose Wisely," *Ensign*, November 2014,
48–49.

29. Dennis B. Neuenschwander, "Holy Place, Sacred Space," *Ensign*,
May 2003.

30. Becky Edwards, "Are you putting on the full armor of God
every day? Holy habits are the key."

Prayer ~~ Scripture Study ~~ Meals ~~ Home Evening ~~ Traditions

Fortify Your Fortress

Fortify Your Fortress

"The Lord is my rock, and my fortress, and my deliverer . . . my buckler, and the horn of my salvation, and my high tower."

—Psalm 18:2

Since earliest times, fortresses have been built to protect feuding kingdoms from invading armies. Because vulnerable peasants were too poor to adequately defend themselves, the king provided a place of refuge for all his subjects. Formidable castle walls ensured safety for prince and pauper, and inside those physical enclosures there was *peace, power, and protection.*

And since the beginning of time, the Lord has encouraged the building of religious fortresses to protect precious loved ones from the invasive attacks of Satan and his allies. Because vulnerable stripling warriors are not adequately prepared to defend themselves, the parents of each private castle must provide a place of refuge for their children. A formidable family fortress ensures safety for parent and child; and within these spiritual enclosures, there is *peace, power, and protection.*

One of the most formidable fortresses built today is the temple. As the grand symbol of our faith, the temple stands as a beacon of light in an ever-darkening world. It is a sanctuary from the wickedness that surrounds us. The temple is a house of God—literally. We attend the temple to be near Him, and I bear my witness that He is there. Within those sacred walls, covenants are made that connect the past, present, and future and bind families eternally. Go to the temple often. It is a place of *peace, power, and protection.*

Next to the temple, "only the home can compare . . . in sacredness" (Bible Dictionary, "Temple"). What an impressive, intriguing, and intimidating phrase. If I were making this comparison, I suppose I would have said, "Only our church buildings, the Conference Center, the Missionary Training Center, or other religious buildings can compare with the temple." But the Bible Dictionary plainly states, "*Only the home* can compare with the temple in sacredness" (emphasis added).

So how do we create that kind of home? It is a perplexing question that troubled me for some time. Somehow, attaining the temple's holiness in my home seemed so far from reality.

Where Heaven and Earth Meet

While studying temple symbolism, my husband discovered that one architectural design for the temple is a circle within a square. The circle is symbolic of heaven or eternity, for with God all things are "one eternal round" (D&C 3:2)—no beginning and no end. The square is symbolic of earth. When referring to our temporal abode, the scriptures often use the term "the four corners of the earth" (Revelation 7:1). Therefore, when a circle is placed within a square, it represents a place where *heaven and earth meet.*

The Bountiful Utah Temple is rich in this motif: the fence surrounding the temple grounds, the planter boxes in the parking lot, the temple doors. Everywhere, there are circles within squares. As the intersection of temporal and spiritual, the temple truly is a place where *heaven and earth meet.*

A circle—like the early stone enclosures that provided protection from invaders—is meant to keep some things in and keep some things out. Our pioneer ancestors understood this defense strategy. At the end of each day on the trail, they circled their wagons for protection against prowlers and predators, and when they reached the Salt Lake Valley, they built forts *around* their settlements.

Captain Moroni also understood the need for safe enclosures when he commenced "in digging up heaps of earth *round* about all the cities, throughout all the land which was possessed by the Nephites. . . .Thus [he] did prepare strongholds against the coming of their enemies, *round* about every city in all the land" (Alma 50:1, 6; emphasis added).

And when the ancient soldier girded his loins, he was encircled with a girdle that held up his tunic and was prepared to fight the enemy. Thus, another meaning of gird is to "surround or encircle."[1] Spiritually speaking, to gird our loins is to encircle in truth and prepare to battle evil.

Circles enclose and define. They are defenses against the "devilish diversions"[2] lurking just outside their bounds. They provide *peace, power, and protection.*

But what do circles and squares have to do with building family fortresses? And how do we go about making our homes a bit of heaven on earth? For me, the answers came quite unexpectedly while gathering for family prayer one day. Kneeling in a circle on the new area rug in our living room, I noticed that we were forming a circle within a square.

For nearly thirty years, we had been performing this simple act without being aware of its symbolism.

Likewise, when we gather *around* the table to share a meal or *around* the room for family scripture study, family home evening, or other family rituals—inside the *four corners* of our homes—that is where *heaven and earth meet.* There is security in those family circles. They act as a kind of shield or enclosure, keeping vice out and virtue in. We even have Christ's promise that "where two or three are gathered together in my name . . . there will I be in the midst of them" (D&C 6:32).

And that is how our home becomes as sacred as the temples. Gather often. You can more easily keep Satan out as you consistently invite Christ in. There is *peace, power, and protection* in circling your family.

Temples Tie Heaven and Earth Together

Elder Gary E. Stevenson explained, "There exists a righteous unity between the temple and the home. Understanding the eternal nature of the temple will draw you to your family; understanding the eternal nature of the family will draw you to the temple."[3] And President Boyd K. Packer taught, "The ultimate end of all activity in the Church is to see a husband and his wife and their children happy at home, protected by the principles and laws of the gospel, sealed safely in the covenants of the everlasting priesthood."[4] "The temple is the knot that ties heaven and earth together."[5]

The Book of Mormon people who came to listen to King Benjamin's final address must have understood this connection, for they "pitched their tents round about the temple, every man having his tent with the door thereof towards the temple"

(Mosiah 2:6). We would do well to follow their examples, always keeping the doors of our hearts and homes toward this sacred structure. Both the temple and the home are places where scriptures, prayer, and religious rituals bring heaven and earth together.

Keeping Your Fortress Uncontaminated

Ultimately, "heaven is a continuation of the ideal home."[6] Or, as President Thomas S. Monson stated, "A happy home is but an earlier heaven."[7] Truly, "happiness is homemade"[8] and "is most likely to be achieved when founded upon the teachings of the Lord Jesus Christ."[9]

Therefore, we must religiously build barriers of protection against the demons who seek to destroy our domiciles. Our homes must become spiritual harbors set apart from the "moral dry rot"[10] that afflicts society. Do not surrender your sanctuary to Satan by allowing "evil influences to contaminate your own special spiritual environment."[11]

When the Nephite nation was threatened with decay from within, and the affairs of the people were "exceedingly precarious and dangerous" (Alma 46:7), Captain Moroni immediately came up with a plan to purge the festering corruption from the land. He "rent his coat; and . . . took a piece thereof, and wrote upon it—In memory of our God, our religion, and freedom, and our peace, our wives, and our children" (Alma 46:12). Then, holding aloft this banner, he marched from city to city, rallying support for the "cause of the Christians" (Alma 46:16). And "the people came running together with their armor girded about their loins, rending their garments . . . as a covenant, that they would not forsake the Lord their God; or . . . transgress the commandments" (verse 21). When they were at last victorious against the prevailing evil, Moroni "caused the title of liberty to be hoisted upon every tower which was in all the land" (verse 36). Raising that banner was a constant reminder of their covenant with the Lord and their determination to remain faithful (see verses 20–24).

A few years ago, my family participated in a Church-sponsored handcart trek. Before leaving, we fashioned a family banner to be carried with us. It had several symbols, including a large circle within a square, providing visual reminders of our gospel standards. Soon after returning home, we had a family home evening where we signed our names on small pieces of paper and pinned them to the banner in witness of our determination to always stay true to our covenants and our Christian cause.

Trusted leaders in God's army know that passively sitting on the sidelines will not save their children. They know that they must confidently raise the standard of truth in their homes and courageously lead the march against destructive and imposing forces. Furthermore, they know that "the most important . . . work [they] will ever do will be within the walls of [their] own homes."[12] Protecting the home front is fundamental to keeping children free from Satan's corrosive clutches and winning this war with wickedness.

Creating a Holy House

During the dedicatory prayer of the Kirtland Temple, the Prophet Joseph pleaded, "And we ask thee, Holy Father, that thy servants may go forth from this house armed with thy power, and that thy name may be upon them, and thy glory be round about them, and thine angels have charge over them" (D&C 109:22). These were the glorious blessings he sought for those who visited God's holy house, and they can be the blessings for our houses as well, if we do our part.

In conference, Dennis B. Neuenschwander counseled,

> Amidst the bustle of the secular world, with its certain uncertainty, there must be places that offer spiritual refuge, renewal, hope, and peace. There are indeed such places. They are both holy and sacred. They are places where we meet the divine and find the Spirit of the Lord. . . . The importance of holy places and sacred space . . . can hardly be overestimated.
>
> Great personal preparation is required for us to receive the spiritual benefit of standing in holy places. Holy places and sacred space are also distinguished by the sacrifice they require. Elder M. Russell Ballard has taught that "the word sacrifice means literally 'to make sacred,' or 'to render sacred.'" The words sacred and sacrifice come from the same root. One may not have the sacred without first sacrificing something for it. . . . Sacrifice sanctifies the sacred.[13]

The scriptures repeatedly warn of the need to stand in holy places, and it is becoming increasingly imperative that our homes are holy places. We have been admonished to "establish a house, even a house of prayer, a house of fasting, a house of faith, a house of learning, a house of glory, a house of order, a house of God" (D&C 88:119). God wants us to create "spiritual mansions"[14]—sacred, holy places where our children are safe from the world to learn and practice righteous principles.

What, then, would you be willing to sacrifice to make your home a holy place with sacred space? This question deserves serious self-reflection. "Sometimes we are tempted to let our lives be governed more by convenience than by covenant. It is not always convenient to live gospel standards. . . . But there is no spiritual power in living by convenience. . . . We must never give up our individual and family quest for eternal life."[15]

Prioritizing Our Lives

As President Ezra Taft Benson taught, "When we put God first, all other things fall into their proper place or drop out of our lives. Our love of the Lord will govern the claims for our affection, the demands on our time, the interests we pursue, and the order of our priorities."[16] I plead with you to prayerfully analyze your life. Can anything be simplified, minimized, consolidated, or eliminated to create a "house of glory . . . a house of God" (D&C 88:119)?

> Remember, remember that it is upon the rock of our Redeemer, who is Christ, the Son of God, that ye must build your foundation; that when the devil shall send forth his mighty winds, yea, his shafts in the whirlwind, yea, when all his hail and his mighty storm shall beat upon you, it shall have no power over you to drag you down to the gulf of misery and endless wo, because of the rock upon which ye are built, which is a sure foundation, a foundation whereon if men build they cannot fall. (Helaman 5:12)

In a letter to Church members in 1999, the First Presidency urged parents "to devote their best efforts to the teaching and rearing of their children in gospel principles which will keep them close to the Church. The home is the basis of a righteous life, and no other instrumentality can take its place or fulfill its essential functions in carrying forward this God-given responsibility. We counsel parents and children to give highest priority to family prayer, family home evening, gospel study and instruction, and wholesome family activities."[17]

Religious Rituals

What we do in our homes does make a difference, and how we raise our impressionable young children will, to a great extent, determine the course of their lives. If we want to raise valiant latter-day warriors, we must lead the way. "If we want our children to pray, we must show them by example through family prayer. If we want our children to read the scriptures, they need to see the scriptures being read in the family. The factor that has the greatest effect on private religious behavior is family worship, meaning that the family is having regular family prayer, family scripture study, and family home evening."[18]

Don't become discouraged, however, if these repeated rituals are not producing immediate results. It may take a long time before you reap what you have sown. Day after day after day—for more than four years—the Chinese bamboo plant is carefully tended with no visible sign of success. During this time, all the growth is in the ground, forming a massive root structure that will eventually support an incredible spurt of growth. Suddenly, in just six weeks it rises eighty to ninety feet! "If the Chinese bamboo plant immediately shot up 90 feet in the first year, one strong wind would blow it down. By growing deep before it grows tall, it gains the strength it needs to withstand the force of heavy winds."[19]

Likewise, your daily devotionals may seem void of noticeable outcomes, but you never know what testimonies may be growing just below the surface. "Patience is faith in action. Patience is emotional diligence. It's the willingness to suffer inside so that others can grow."[20] Furthermore, "Lasting growth starts on the inside of people. It's difficult to see that change is taking place, but this is a necessary process. The growing they do on the inside creates strength of character and conviction."[21]

Not only are we sometimes impatient for our children to mature spiritually, but we are also sometimes a little too quick to compare our family to someone else's—our sister's, our mother's, our neighbor's, our best friend's, or our coworker's. But we must be careful about comparing, as Elder Robert D. Hales cautioned, "When you . . . think that someone has a perfect family, you just do not know them well enough."[22] I often reflect on this advice when I am feeling inferior or inadequate.

Don't lose faith because of your failings—we all have them. "Do what you can, with what you have, where you are."[23] Constantly looking back and focusing on regrets doesn't allow you to see the possibilities that lie ahead. Just because you lose a battle doesn't mean you've lost the war. Even the best generals lose an encounter now and then.

Never Leave a Wounded Warrior

And don't lose faith when a child fails. As President James E. Faust so lovingly reminded, "Some. . . children could tax even Solomon's wisdom and Job's patience."[24] Elder Hales also said, "We should never let the searching and struggling of our children make us waver or lose our faith in the Lord. . . . We must never, out of anger, lock the door of our home or our heart to our children. Like the prodigal son, our children need to know that when they come to themselves they can turn to us for love and counsel."[25]

Through the parables of the lost sheep, the lost coin, and the prodigal son, the Savior taught that we should never stop searching for the one who is lost. After all, God doesn't give up on us. There is great joy in heaven over he that "was lost, and is found" (Luke 15:32). Even in the midst of our grief and despair over a child who wanders, we must not lose hope. "In the battle of life, the adversary takes enormous numbers of prisoners. . . . Every soul confined to a concentration camp of sin and guilt has a key to the gate. The adversary cannot hold them if they know how to use it. The key is labeled Repentance. The twin principles of repentance and forgiveness exceed in strength the awesome power of the adversary."[26]

An important tenet of war is to never leave a wounded warrior. Likewise, when our own precious soldiers fall, we must gently, lovingly, and continuously implement a plan to save them, even if that means simply watching and waiting, hoping and praying. Remember the bamboo plant—you never know when your rescue efforts will produce results.

Be Not Weary in Well Doing

Elder David A. Bednar likened the ongoing challenges of raising children to a painting of a wheat field that hangs in his office:

> [It] is a vast collection of individual brushstrokes—none of which in isolation is very interesting or impressive. In fact,

if you stand close to the canvas, all you can see is a mass of seemingly unrelated and unattractive streaks of yellow and gold and brown paint. However, as you gradually move away from the canvas, all of the individual brushstrokes combine together and produce a magnificent landscape of a wheat field. Many ordinary, individual brushstrokes work together to create a captivating and beautiful painting.

Each family prayer, each episode of family scripture study, and each family home evening is a brushstroke on the canvas of our souls. No one event may appear to be very impressive or memorable. But just as the yellow and gold and brown strokes of paint complement each other and produce an impressive masterpiece, so our consistency in doing seemingly small things can lead to significant spiritual results. "Wherefore, be not weary in well-doing, for ye are laying the foundation of a great work. And out of small things proceedeth that which is great" (D&C 64:33).[27]

Building a holy house and a righteous regiment of latter-day warriors is not easy. It takes time; it takes effort. It uses up precious personal energy and further complicates our already complicated lives. But I promise it is worth it. *Nothing* you do is more important. A more fixed focus on our family's spiritual well-being will keep the metaphorical weeds and dirt and clutter out of our lives, strengthen the stripling soldiers in our charge, fortify our fortresses, and keep the proverbial predators at bay. These sometimes seemingly insignificant efforts will produce everlasting results. "Peace will prevail in your life. That peace won't come from the outside world. It will come from within your home, from within your family, from within your own heart. . . . You will find peace in the turmoil around you and strength to resist temptations."[28]

Upgrade Your Battle Plan

Make no mistake about it—we are at war! It was prophesied that in our day, "Michael . . . shall gather together his armies, even the hosts of heaven. And the devil shall gather together his armies; even the hosts of hell, and shall come up to battle against Michael and his armies. And then cometh the battle of the great God" (D&C 88:112–14).

God has a battle plan. It is a grand, majestic, exalted plan— "the plan of salvation" (Moses 6:62), "the plan of redemption" (Alma 12:30), "the plan of mercy" (Alma 42:15), or the "great plan of happiness" (Alma 42:8). His plan provides a way for each of us to return safely to Him and live as families eternally. It includes impressive counterattacks on Satan's evil schemes and the eventual overthrow of his earthly empire. Lovingly, it includes a Savior who rescues the wounded, the weary, the oppressed, the down-trodden, and the heavy-laden. His plan is perfect. Failure to follow the plan only increases our own sorrow and suffering, but when His plan becomes our plan, it eliminates the risk of spiritual injury.

Now is the time to "upgrade our [own] battle plans."[29] Many of the strategies that worked for our parents and grandparents may no longer work for us. "As the forces [of sin] around us increase in intensity, whatever spiritual strength was once sufficient will not be enough."[30]

We are being bombarded with evil, and Satan is making an all-out assault on the family that will tear at the testimonies of the best of us. I believe the day will come when our children's spiritual safety will depend on the depth and breadth of those testimonies and the strength of their own spiritual armor. That armor is not built by doing the fun things of life. As President Gordon B. Hinckley so aptly stated, "You cannot refine the substance of character from the husks of pleasure."[31]

Do your children have deep and abiding testimonies of Jesus Christ and His restored gospel? Do they know that Satan is real and extremely powerful and persuasive? And do they understand the importance of clinging tightly to righteous principles if they hope to triumph over evil? In a world ravaged by war, children need to know that "real disciples absorb the fiery darts of the adversary by holding aloft the quenching shield of faith with one hand, while holding to the iron rod with the other (see Ephesians 6:16; 1 Nephi 15:24; D&C 27:17). There should be no mistaking; it will take both hands!"[32]

Our children also need to know that as we valiantly endure, we have the assurance that "they that be with us are more than they that be with them" (2 Kings 6:16). Christ will be on our right hand and on our left hand, and His angels *round* about us to bear us up (see D&C 84:88; emphasis added). And we have the glorious promise that "to him that overcometh will I grant to sit with me in my throne" (Revelation 3:21), where we will be "*encircled* about eternally in the arms of his love" (2 Nephi 1:15; emphasis added). "Shall we not go on in so great a cause?" (D&C 128:22).

"Build your walls! Guard your gates!"[33] Arm your soldiers and fortify your fortress! "The gospel of Jesus Christ and the covenants we have made inevitably cast us as combatants in the eternal contest between truth and error. There is no middle ground in [this] contest."[34]

Parenthood unavoidably propels us to the prestigious rank of lifelong commissioned officers in this conflict, and God expects us to stand boldly at the head of our own mini militia in defending truth and right and protecting our stripling warriors from Satan's attacks. As His trusted emissaries and veteran crusaders, it is our sacred duty to love and lead, provide and protect, and teach and train the next generation of soldiers—a charge from which we must not shirk or shrink. Generals in His army do not stop, back down, back off, give in, give up, or walk away. With heaven's help, we can outmaneuver, outsmart, outlast, and outfight this most formidable foe. Surrender is not an option.

When the final struggle has ended and there is no more war, may we triumphantly proclaim as the Apostle Paul, "I have fought a good fight, I have finished my course, I have kept the faith" (2 Timothy 4:7). On to victory!

Notes

1. See "Gird," *Vocabulary*, accessed October 2015, http://www.vocabulary.com/dictionary/gird.

2. M. Russell Ballard, "Guiding Children as They Make Decisions," *Marriage and Family Relations: Participant's Study Guide* (Salt Lake City: Intellectual Reserve, 2000), 65.

3. Gary E. Stevenson, "Sacred Homes, Sacred Temples," *Ensign*, May 2009.

4. Boyd K. Packer, "And a Little Child Shall Lead Them," *Ensign*, May 2012.

5. Bruce C. Hafen, "The Temple and the Natural Order of Marriage," *Ensign*, September 2015, 41.

6. *Preach My Gospel: A Guide to Missionary Service* (Salt Lake City: Intellectual Reserve, 2004), 85.

7. Thomas S. Monson, "Children Are an Heritage of the Lord," *Marriage and Family Relations, Participant's Study Guide*, 36.

8. Howard W. Hunter, as quoted by LeGrand R. Curtis, "A Table Encircled with Love," *Marriage and Family Relations, Participant's Study Guide*, 52.

9. "The Family—A Proclamation to the World," *Ensign*, November 1995.

10. James E. Faust, "The Greatest Challenge in the World—Good Parenting," *Marriage and Family Relations, Participant's Study Guide*, 49.

11. M. Russell Ballard, "Like a Flame Unquenchable," *Ensign*, May 1999.

12. Harold B. Lee, *Teachings of Presidents of the Church* (Salt Lake City: Intellectual Reserve, 2000), 134; emphasis added.

13. Dennis B. Neuenschwander, "Holy Place, Sacred Space," *Ensign*, May 2003.

14. Ibid.

15. M. Russell Ballard, "Like a Flame Unquenchable."

16. Ezra Taft Benson, "The Great Commandment—Love the Lord," *Ensign*, May 1988.

17. "Letter from the First Presidency," *Liahona*, December 1999.

18. Gene R. Cook, *Raising Up a Family to the Lord* (Salt Lake City: Deseret Book, 1993), 19.

19. Michael Kientz, "The Amazing Chinese Bamboo Plant," *Build Your Walls! Guard Your Gates!*, posted August 13, 2008, https://wallbuilder.wordpress.com/2008/08/13/the-amazing-chinese-bamboo-plant/.

20. Stephen R. Covey, as quoted in "The Chinese bamboo tree: a

parable for parents," *Nurture Mama*, posted January 2010, http://nurturemama.blogspot.com/2010/01/chinese-bamboo-tree-parable-for-parents.html.

21. Michael Kientz, "The Amazing Chinese Bamboo Plant."

22. Robert D. Hales, "Strengthening Families: Our Sacred Duty," *Ensign*, May 1999.

23. Theodore Roosevelt, *Goodreads*, accessed February 28, 2015, http://www.goodreads.com/quotes/188-do-what-you-can-with-what-you-have-where-you.

24. James E. Faust, "The Greatest Challenge in the World—Good Parenting," 50.

25. Robert D. Hales, "Strengthening Families: Our Sacred Duty."

26. Boyd K. Packer, "Our Moral Environment," *Ensign*, May 1992.

27. David A. Bednar, "More Diligent and Concerned at Home," *Ensign*, November 2009.

28. Richard G. Scott, "Make the Exercise of Faith Your First Priority," *Ensign*, November 2014, 93.

29. Becky Edwards, "Are you putting on the full armor of God every day? Holy habits are the key," *Purpose Driven Motherhood*, posted January 7, 2015, http://purposedrivenmotherhood.blogspot.com/2015/01/are-you-putting-on-full-armor-of-god.html.

30. Henry B. Eyring, "'Always,'" *Ensign*, November 1999.

31. Gordon B. Hinckley, *Standing for Something* (New York: Harmony, 2001).

32. Neal A. Maxwell, "Overcome . . . Even As I Also Overcame," *Ensign*, May 1987.

33. Michael Kientz, "The Amazing Chinese Bamboo Plant."

34. Dallin H. Oaks, "Loving Others and Living with Differences," *Ensign*, November 2014, 26.

Prayer~~~Scripture Study~~Meals~~Home Evening~~Traditions~~

Family

The Battlefront

Boom! Boom! The cannons echo; around you lays the gore,
Carnage left by countless battles in this eternal war.
All who ever lived, have been enlisted in this fight—
The fight of good and evil, the fight of wrong and right.
Both sides call to join their ranks, but choose most carefully,
For what you choose will chart your course for all eternity.

On one side stands Debauchery, in all its shades of black,
Complete with subtle battle plans, ready to attack.
His army and his minions and all his tactics too
Are well rehearsed and well played out—they're good at what they do.
He offers lustful wantings, borrowed from the beast;
And pushing self-indulgence tempts, "Come, sit down and feast!"

He is the king of anger, of hate, of apathy;
The captain of the captive, the prince of tyranny.
With artful propaganda, he leads you into sin;
And as you trudge through mud and blood, he chants, "I win! I win!"
He is the master marketer, your heart his quota's goal,
For if he gets your heart, he knows, he also gets your soul.

Yet against this host of clamoring hogs, ready for the fight,
Stands serenely Virtue, clothed in purest white.
And no, she does not stand alone, she has for company,
Faith and Hope and endless love, the love called Charity.
With these march God's army, robed with righteous power,
Led by His sustaining light that guides them every hour.

Throughout millennia this war has raged, and still continues on,
Like night that follows darkening dusk and day that follows dawn.
And still the two sides battle . . . which one will win or lose?
The answer to that question depends on which you choose.
For one alone will triumph; the other will be dead.
Where lies this mighty battlefront? All inside your head.

—Trenton Bowen

Family Battle Plan

"Wherefore, gird up your loins and be prepared.
Behold, the kingdom is yours, and the enemy shall not overcome."

—D&C 38:9

Commit to having family prayer, family scripture study,
and at least one family meal a day.

Commit to having family home evening weekly.

Establish "holy habits" and traditions
that strengthen home and family.

Reduce distractions.
Be wise in your use of technology and extracurricular activities.

Maintain an eternal perspective.

Keep the faith.
Just because you lose a battle does not mean you've lost the war.

Never leave a wounded warrior.

Do not stop, back down, back off, give in, give up, or walk away.
Surrender is not an option.

Fear not.
"I will be on your right hand and on your left . . .
and mine angels round about you, to bear you up."
—D&C 84:88

About the Author

It has been Debbie Bowen's privilege to serve as co-commander in chief, alongside her husband, in raising ten latter-day stripling warriors—six sons and four daughters. Together, they have spent more than three decades teaching and training their little band of soldiers and have had ample opportunity to test the techniques and strategies discussed in this book. As difficult as it can sometimes be, they consider their calling as generals in God's army and their divine mandate to raise righteous children to be their greatest mission and most important battle.